THE PERFECT

EGG

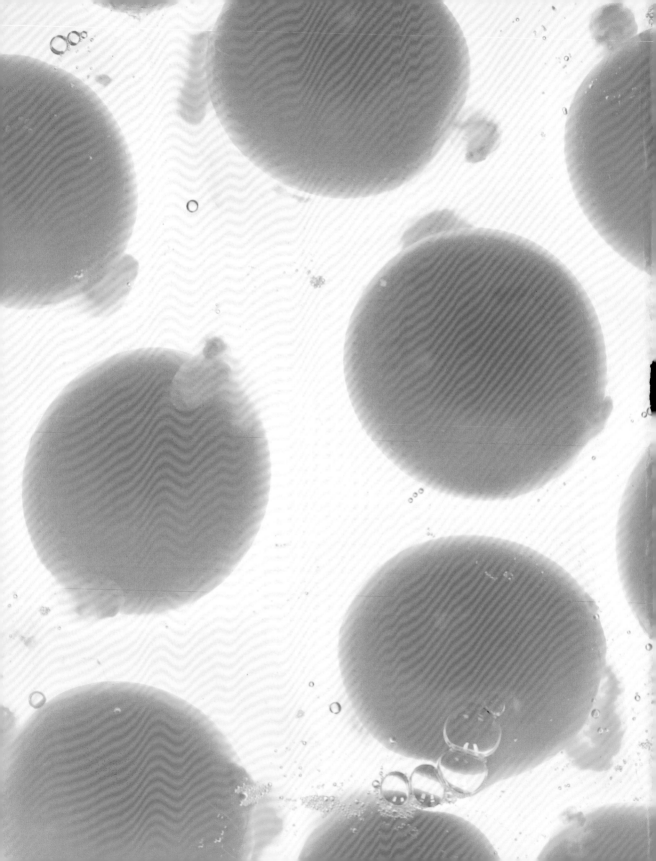

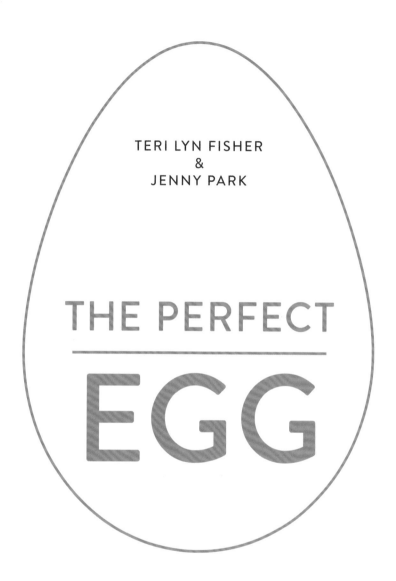

TERI LYN FISHER
&
JENNY PARK

THE PERFECT

EGG

A Fresh Take on Recipes for Morning, Noon, and Night

TEN SPEED PRESS

Berkeley

CONTENTS

INTRODUCTION

Consider the egg, its fragile armor perfectly shaped to protect an essential and versatile food. It delivers flavor, texture, and nutrition, whether standing proudly on its own or playing a crucial role in a myriad of dishes. Itching to bake? Beat a few eggs to aerate them, and then use them to both leaven and give structure to a cake batter. Need to enrich a sauce? Whisk in an egg yolk for flavor and body. Looking to lighten a soufflé? Whip egg whites to beautiful, glossy peaks, then fold them into the soufflé base. Want to silence your growling belly with a protein-packed bite? Cook up an egg on its own for a quick, delicious, and nutritious snack. Most people think of eggs as something to scramble, hard boil, fry over easy, or maybe whisk for a quiche. In *The Perfect Egg*, we explore the universality of this iconic food, in both everyday and more innovative preparations.

Eggs come in a charming array of colors, from bright white, nutty brown, rich green, and light blue to brown and tan speckles on a pale background. Their shells may be thick or thin, their shapes oblong or squat. Chicken eggs are smaller, have a milder flavor, and have a more delicate shell than duck eggs, which typically sport a large, deep-orange yolk and boast a particularly rich flavor. Quail eggs, which are no bigger than a teaspoon, taste similar to chicken eggs, with creamy yolks and soft whites. Our recipes call for all three types of eggs.

Since the 1980s, eggs have been demonized as both high in cholesterol and potential salmonella carriers. More recently, however, advanced research and better sustainability practices have helped to diminish many of the fears surrounding egg consumption. Nowadays, people are beginning to recognize eggs as among the most affordable and widely available sources of protein. They're also easily renewable, are quick and easy to cook, and are dense with nutrients, such as antioxidants, vitamins, and minerals.

In the pages that follow, we describe the different varieties of eggs available, discuss the anatomy of the egg so that you can better understand how each part behaves in a recipe, provide a primer on egg grading, and decode the many descriptive labels found on store cartons. We also share our foolproof techniques for nine common egg preparations, from baked, boiled, and coddled to scrambled and steamed, which you can serve as is or use as building blocks for creating your own dishes. Most importantly, we reveal the recipes for our favorite egg dishes from around the world, which we have organized by time of day or type of treat: morning, snacks, afternoon, night, and sweets.

EGG INFO

ALL ABOUT EGGS

Eggs are so commonplace that we usually just grab a carton at the supermarket without thinking too much about what's inside. And why not? Eggs all look pretty much alike— same color (brown or white), same shape (oval)—and taste pretty much alike. But there are differences, and understanding what they are will help to make you a savvier shopper and cook. We will start off with a brief history of commercial egg production in the United States, which helps to explain why eggs are so widely available, and then describe the most common egg varieties available, how eggs are graded and sized, and how to decode the language you find on an egg carton.

FROM FAMILY FARM TO FACTORY FARM

In the early 1900s, most farm families in America raised at least a few chickens for eggs and, to a much lesser degree, for meat. With the discovery of vitamin D in the early 1920s, the size of the flocks grew as farmers began to mix the vitamin into chicken feed to keep their birds, which traditionally struggled to stay alive during the winter months, fairly healthy year-round. The family chicken flock soon became a welcome source of income, and for the next three decades, the majority of the country's commercial egg industry was the product of relatively small farms. That changed in the 1950s with the growth of the cage system, in which hens were housed in elevated cages to improve production efficiency as well as sanitary conditions through organization and ventilation, a move that initially benefitted both the birds and consumers. Today, the cage system has replaced the farmyard flock as the source of most commercial chicken eggs, with the majority of commercial egg farmers caring for flocks that number in the tens of thousands of birds.

Recently, a growing number of consumers have been passing up the cheaper, less ethically produced cage system eggs (poor-quality feed, growth-inducing drugs, crowded conditions) in favor of more costly free-range or pastured eggs (see page 3) laid by hens that enjoy a more healthful diet (which determines how an egg tastes) and more spacious quarters.

GRADING AND SIZING EGGS

Egg grading follows standards established by the United States Department of Agriculture (USDA) for both the exterior and the interior of the egg. The exterior, or shell, is evaluated for such features as texture, shape, cleanliness, and fissures. A process known as candling, which uses high-intensity light, is used to illuminate the interior, allowing for inspection of such qualities as the firmness and purity of the yolk, the density of the white, and the size of the air cell (see page 7), all of which are key to establishing the freshness of the egg. The USDA employs three egg grades, AA, A, and B, in descending order of quality.

AA: Has a bright, plump yolk; a tight, firm white; and an unblemished, unbroken shell.

A: Has a bright, plump yolk; a moderately tight, firm white; and an unblemished, unbroken shell.

B: Has a flatter, wider yolk; a thin, runny white; and a shell that is unbroken but may be stained.

Once eggs are graded, they are sorted according to size. The established sizes are classified by the USDA according to the minimum net weight affirmed in ounces per dozen. Here we have listed the different sizes available to the public, from smallest to largest, along with the average weights for both a single egg dozen.

PEEWEE: 1.25 ounces each and 15 ounces per dozen

MEDIUM: 1.75 ounces each and 21 ounces per dozen

EXTRA LARGE: 2.25 ounces each and 27 ounces per dozen

SMALL: 1.5 ounces each and 18 ounces per dozen

LARGE: 2 ounces each and 24 ounces per dozen

JUMBO: 2.5 ounces each and 30 ounces per dozen

DECODING EGG CARTONS

Egg cartons packed in a USDA-inspected plant must always include a "pack date," which is the day the eggs were cleaned, graded, and loaded into the carton. It is a three-digit number on one end of the carton, and it represents the consecutive day of the year. For example, if the eggs were packed on January 1, the date would read 001; and on December 31, it would be 365. Although not required by law, a "sell by date" is usually stamped near the pack date. It includes the month, day, and sometimes the year, such as Aug 10 | 14. In USDA-inspected plants, the sell by date cannot be more than 30 days after the pack date. What follows are some of the other common labels you will encounter on egg cartons.

CAGE-FREE: Eggs laid by chickens that are uncaged. Typically, they can only roam indoors, such as in a barn, and the quarters are often extremely crowded.

FREE-RANGE: Eggs laid by chickens that have some access to the outdoors, though a number of restrictions can apply and standards typically vary from farm to farm.

PASTURED: Eggs laid by chickens that can freely roam the farmyard, foraging and living the "natural" life of a chicken. These eggs are generally produced on small farms.

ORGANIC: Eggs laid by chickens fed an organic diet, raised without vaccines or antibiotics, and allowed access to the outdoors.

VEGETARIAN: Eggs laid by chickens on a strict vegetarian diet. Hens are by nature omnivores—in fact, they will eat almost anything—so they must be watched closely to ensure that their eggs remain as labeled.

OMEGA-3 EGGS: Eggs laid by chickens fed a diet high in omega-3 fatty acids. Some believe that eggs with a high concentration of omega-3s contribute to reducing the risk of cardiovascular disease.

PASTEURIZED: Eggs that have been exposed to a time- and temperature-controlled water bath to kill any potentially harmful microorganisms, such as bacteria and viruses.

EGG VARIETIES

Chicken eggs are the most commonly consumed egg variety in the United States, but the eggs of many other birds are also eaten here and elsewhere in the world. Here is an egg sampler that we hope will inspire you to go beyond the chicken egg.

QUAIL · CHICKEN · DUCK · TURKEY

QUAIL: The smallest of the commercially available egg varieties, quail eggs are about 1 inch long and ¾ inch in diameter and weigh just a ½ ounce. The shell ranges from light tan to brown and is heavily speckled. The yolks are often paired with raw ground meat for tartare preparations or with raw oysters or sea urchin for seafood shooters, and the whole eggs are delicious hard boiled. If cooking quail eggs, keep in mind that they require only a fraction of the time over heat of chicken eggs. Look for quail eggs in specialty markets, Asian markets, and some farmers' markets.

CHICKEN: The average chicken egg is about 2 inches long and 1 inch in diameter and weighs roughly 2½ ounces. Its shell may be blue, green, brown, or white, depending on the breed of chicken, though the color does not affect the flavor of the egg. You can easily find chicken eggs at supermarkets, convenience stores, and at many farmers' markets, or you can sometimes buy them directly from a local farm.

DUCK: Increasingly popular in home kitchens, duck eggs have blue or white shells. They are great to use in place of chicken eggs for baking cakes and quick breads, as their bright, creamy, high-fat yolks and high-protein whites create a richer, lighter, moister result. Be careful not to overcook them or they will turn rubbery because of their high protein content. The average duck egg is about 2½ inches long and 1¼ inches in diameter and weighs about 3¼ ounces, so is roughly 30 percent larger than a chicken egg. You can purchase duck eggs at farmers' markets, Asian markets, some high-end grocery stores, from local farmers, or online.

TURKEY: The average turkey egg is about 3 inches long and 1¾ inches in diameter and weighs a scant 4 ounces, so is about twice the size of a medium chicken egg. The shell is often speckled and ranges from light brown to cream. You can find turkey eggs at some farmers' markets, but your best bet is to visit a local turkey farm.

GOOSE

EMU

OSTRICH

GOOSE: This large egg averages about 3½ inches long and 2 inches in diameter and weighs about 5 ounces. The shells are usually matte ivory and quite sturdy, and the large, richly flavored yolks are a vivid yellow. Goose eggs have a higher ratio of yolk to white than chicken eggs, so if you opt to trade out whole chicken eggs for whole goose eggs in a cake recipe, the crumb will be denser. A local farmer is your best source for goose eggs.

EMU: The second largest of all bird eggs, the emu egg, which weighs in at about 1½ pounds, averages about 6 inches long and 3½ inches in diameter. Emu eggs are available at some farmers' markets (admittedly rarely), from local emu farmers, or online. A single emu egg is equivalent to about 14 large chicken eggs and can feed up to 14 people.

OSTRICH: The largest of the eggs, the ostrich egg averages 6 inches long and 5 inches in diameter and may weigh as much as 3 pounds. Its cream-colored shell is thick and glossy and so hard that you'll need a hammer to break it. Ostrich eggs are difficult to source, with a local ostrich farmer and the Internet as your best chances for tracking them down. A single ostrich egg is equivalent to about 16 large chicken eggs and can feed up to 16 people.

NOTE: Only three varieties of eggs—the most popularly used varieties in the United States—are used in the recipes that follow. Most often we are calling for large chicken eggs, which appear simply as "eggs" in our ingredients lists. In a few recipes, we specify medium eggs. When quail and duck eggs are used, we specify the variety.

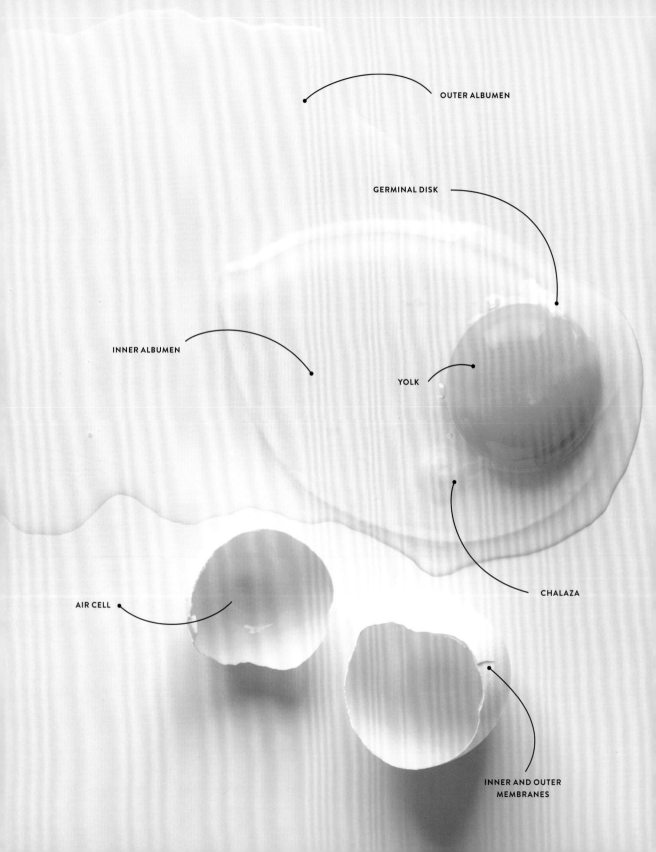

OUTER ALBUMEN

GERMINAL DISK

INNER ALBUMEN

YOLK

CHALAZA

AIR CELL

INNER AND OUTER
MEMBRANES

ANATOMY OF AN EGG

Here we break down the egg to show you its primary components and how each of them contributes to the whole.

SHELL: Made up primarily of calcium carbonate, the egg's outermost layer is porous, allowing both air and moisture to pass through. That means that over time, an egg will absorb odors and flavors and lose moisture. A super thin coating sheaths the shell to help prevent dust particles and bacteria from penetrating. Because eggshells are high in calcium and vitamin D, they can be crushed into a fine powder and added to homemade cosmetics for a topical application, or to smoothies or baked goods to enrich the diet.

INNER AND OUTER MEMBRANES: These thin sacs of transparent protein surround the albumen to protect the egg from bacterial infiltration and excessive loss of moisture—acting as the second line of defense after the shell. You can sometimes see them when you look at the inside of a freshly cracked shell. When eggs are boiled, these membranes become opaque and also quite sturdy, as they are partially made of keratin, the same protein component found in human hair.

AIR CELL: After an egg is laid, a small pocket of air forms between the inner and outer membrane at the broader end of the shell. The smaller this air cell is, the fresher the egg. That's because as the egg ages, moisture lost through the shell is replaced with air.

CHALAZA: This thick, white, ropelike strand, which is affixed to both ends of the yolk and to the white, is most prominent in very fresh eggs, gradually fading as eggs age. The job of the chalaza is to keep the yolk centered. Once eggs are cooked, it blends into the albumen and yolk, becoming undetectable.

ALBUMEN: The white of the egg, the albumen is an important source of protein and vitamin B2. It is composed primarily of protein, with only traces of fat and no cholesterol. The tighter and thicker the albumen, the fresher the egg.

VITELLINE MEMBRANE: This thin membrane is similar to the inner and outer membranes, but it encases only the yolk, rather than the white and yolk. Very sturdy when an egg is fresh, it loses its strength as the egg ages.

GERMINAL DISK: This small, white spot on the surface of the yolk provides a channel to the center of the yolk to facilitate fertilization. If the egg has been fertilized, this spot is where the embryo will grow.

YOLK: The yolk is high in cholesterol and contains almost all of the fat in the egg. But it also carries almost as much protein as the white as well as several vitamins and minerals, among them vitamins A, D, B6, B12, K, calcium, phosphorus, and iron. The color of the yolk depends on the diet of the bird that laid the egg.

EGGS 101

BASICS

COOKING TECHNIQUES

Here are the most common methods for preparing eggs. These simple recipes will help you become more familiar and comfortable with cooking eggs, so that in time, you will use them as building blocks to create your own dishes. Most of the methods that follow yield a single serving, but the measurements can easily be increased to make more servings.

BAKED: Crack 1 egg into a lightly buttered ramekin and spoon 1 or 2 tablespoons of heavy cream over the top. Bake in a preheated 325°F oven for 10 to 12 minutes, until the white is opaque and has just set and the yolk is somewhat runny. Season with salt and pepper and serve hot.

BOILED: Pour water to a depth of 3 inches into a saucepan and bring to a slow boil over medium-high heat. Using a ladle or spoon, gently lower the eggs, one at a time, into the pan, taking care to keep them in a single layer to avoid crowding. Bring the water back to a slow boil and cook according to the following guidelines for the doneness you prefer: 4½ minutes for soft boiled, 7 minutes for medium boiled, and 10 minutes for hard boiled. Meanwhile, prepare a bowl of ice water. When the eggs are ready, carefully transfer them to the ice water, and then let the eggs cool until they can be handled. The ice-water bath will halt the cooking and will keep the bright yellow yolks from turning green. Boiled eggs can be stored in an airtight container in the refrigerator for up to 5 days. Always store them in the shell for maximum freshness.

CODDLED: Put no more than 3 eggs into a heatproof bowl, pour 4 cups boiling water over them, and let stand for 10 minutes. Retrieve the eggs from the water and dry their shells with a clean kitchen towel. Using the back of a teaspoon gently tap the top of the shell (either end—the narrow or the broad—will do), peel it away, and scoop out the egg with the spoon.

FRENCH OMELET: A traditional French omelet is cooked in clarified butter (because it has a high smoke point), folded into thirds, and has a slightly runny center and no browning on the outside. To make a traditional French omelet, crack 3 eggs into a bowl and whisk together until frothy. Heat 2 tablespoons unsalted, clarified butter in a nonstick skillet over medium heat. When the butter is hot, add the eggs and stir them in small circles with a fork or rubber spatula as they cook. Continue to stir the eggs for about 3 minutes until they are mostly cooked but still quite soft and somewhat runny. Gently smooth the surface of the eggs and place the desired filling, such as herbs or cheese, in the center. Fold the omelet into thirds, starting with the side closest to you, folding it over the filling toward the far side of the pan, and then tilting the skillet away from you to continue to roll and fold the omelet, closed side down, onto the plate. Season with salt and freshly ground black pepper and serve hot.

For a country omelet, proceed as directed for a French omelet but allow the eggs to cook for 2 to 3 minutes longer, until lightly brown on the bottom, before filling, and then fold the omelette in half instead of the trifold.

FRIED: Heat 2 tablespoons of unsalted butter in a nonstick skillet over medium-high heat. Crack 1 egg into a small bowl and gently tip it out into the hot skillet. Let the egg cook for 2 to 3 minutes, then tilt the skillet away from you so that the egg slides to the far edge, near the rim of the pan, and snap your wrist to flip the egg, or use a spatula to turn it. For an over-easy egg, cook for about 30 seconds on the second side before finishing. For an over-medium egg, cook for about 1 minute before finishing. For an over-hard egg, cook for about 2 minutes before finishing. To finish the egg, flip it a second time and cook for 30 seconds to 1 minute longer before tipping it out onto a plate. Season with salt and freshly ground black pepper and serve hot.

For sunny-side up fried eggs, fry eggs in a hot buttered skillet over medium high heat for 4 to 5 minutes or until the edges of the whites begin to crisp and turn golden brown. Carefully tip the eggs onto a plate and serve.

POACHED: Crack 1 egg into a ramekin or small bowl. Pour water to a depth of 4 inches into a saucepan, bring to a boil over medium-high heat, and add 2 teaspoons of white wine vinegar. Using a whisk or wooden spoon, stir the water briskly in one direction, creating a small whirlpool in the center. The vinegar and whirlpool help to keep the egg white (albumen) tight around the yolk. Slide the egg into the center of the whirlpool, cover the pan, and immediately transfer the pan to a cool surface. Let the egg stand for 4 minutes for a very runny yolk or 6 minutes for a firmer, creamy yolk. Using a slotted spoon, retrieve the egg, blot the bottom on a paper towel, and slide onto a plate. Season with salt and freshly ground black pepper and serve hot.

PRESERVED (SALTED): When preserved eggs are cooked, they have a creamy white, a dense yolk, and an appealing briny flavor. Gently wipe the shells of 8 raw eggs with a damp cloth, checking each egg carefully to make sure the shell is not cracked, and place the eggs in a large jar or bowl. In a bowl, stir together 5 cups of warm water, 3 cups of kosher salt, and 1 cup of sugar until the salt and sugar dissolve. Let cool to room temperature. Pour the liquid over the eggs and cover the jar or bowl tightly. Place in a cool, dry spot for 30 to 45 days; the longer the eggs remain in the brine, the saltier they will be. To use, rinse the eggs and then boil or steam for 10 to 12 minutes.

SCRAMBLED: Crack 3 eggs into a bowl, whisk together until frothy, and then whisk in ¼ cup whole milk (to produce creamier, fluffier eggs). Heat 2 tablespoons of unsalted butter in a nonstick skillet, over medium heat. Add the eggs to the skillet and leave for 1 minute without disturbing them. Using a heatproof rubber spatula, gently push the eggs into the center of the skillet, letting the excess liquid run out to the sides. Slowly stir, push, and turn the eggs until large curds form. When the eggs are as firm as you like them, tilt them out onto a plate, season with salt and freshly ground black pepper, and serve hot.

STEAMED: Crack 3 eggs into a bowl, whisk together until frothy, and then whisk in ½ cup of stock (any kind is fine). Divide the eggs evenly between two 6-ounce ramekins, filling each ramekin about three-fourths full. Bring water to a simmer in a steamer pan over medium-high heat. Place the steamer rack over, not touching, the water, and then place the ramekins on the rack, spacing them at least a ½ inch apart. Cover the steamer and steam over medium-low heat for 12 to 15 minutes, until the stock remains clear when you gently pull the eggs away from the sides of a ramekin. Serve hot.

HANDLING AND STORAGE

To keep eggs as fresh as possible and to avoid foodborne illness, you must handle and store them with care. These simple safety measures will ensure your cache of eggs is safe to eat.

HANDLING: Always handle eggs with clean hands to avoid any cross-contamination. Also, when possible, crack them into a bowl before adding them to a pan or to other ingredients, so that you can inspect them for freshness. A fresh egg will have a tight white and a plump, bright yolk.

STORAGE: Refrigerate eggs at 40°F or below (the recommended refrigerator temperature is 35°F to 38°F) in their carton to prevent them from absorbing odors or coming in contact with bacteria. Always store them large end up and keep them on a refrigerator shelf rather than in the egg holder on the door where the temperature can fluctuate. For the best quality, use them within 3 weeks of purchase.

LEFTOVERS: Raw eggs yolks can be stored in an airtight container in the refrigerator for up to 3 days. Before sealing the container, pour enough water over the unbroken, raw yolks to cover the surface completely to keep them moist, then drain off the water before using the yolks. Store raw egg whites the same way but omit the water. Store boiled eggs in their shells in the refrigerator for up to 1 week. Refrigerate leftover cooked egg dishes for no more than 4 days.

SALMONELLA: Although rare, salmonella, a group of bacteria that is transferred to an egg by an infected chicken, either through the yolk and white during the egg's development or through the porous shell, is the most common cause of egg-related illness in the United States. The incidence of salmonella in eggs is low, however, and most people infected with the bacteria overcome the symptoms (stomach cramps, diarrhea) with no further problems within a few days. People at the greatest risk for severe illness are older people, pregnant women, young children, and anyone with a compromised immune system. To limit the possibility of infection, always keep eggs refrigerated and thoroughly wash all utensils, vessels, and surfaces that have been exposed to raw eggs with hot water and soap. Anyone in one of the high-risk groups noted above should avoid eggs that are not fully cooked, that is, that have not been held at a temperature of 140°F for at least 3½ minutes or cooked to a temperature of 160°F. That includes coddled, soft-boiled, and poached eggs as well as any preparations that contain raw eggs, such as mayonnaise.

MAYONNAISE

AIOLI

EGG BUTTER

HOLLANDAISE SAUCE

BÉARNAISE SAUCE

CRÈME ANGLAISE

SABAYON

SAUCES AND CONDIMENTS

Making your own sauces and condiments can seem like a daunting task, especially since you can easily buy the premade stuff with a quick trip to the grocery store. In the following recipes, we show you just how easy it is to make your own popular egg-based sauces, like rich and luscious hollandaise, as well as condiments like a simple and fresh basic mayonnaise. We will also show you how to make a couple sauces and condiments you may not be familiar with like a delicious egg-butter and a sweet and foamy sabayon.

MAYONNAISE

2 eggs

2½ teaspoons Dijon mustard

2 tablespoons freshly squeezed lemon juice

1 cup vegetable oil

Salt

Makes about 1½ cups

Most people buy mayonnaise and have a strong brand preference, depending on the desired level of tang (delivered by vinegar) or creaminess (from the egg-to-oil ratio). What many of these people don't realize is that making mayonnaise at home is incredibly easy and fast, plus when you make it yourself, you can customize it to your taste.

Whisk together the eggs, mustard, and lemon juice in a bowl. While whisking constantly, add the oil drop by drop at first until the mixture begins to thicken, and then in a slow, steady stream. Continue whisking until the oil is fully incorporated and the mixture is smooth and thickened. Whisk in salt to taste.

The mayonnaise will keep in an airtight container in the refrigerator for up to 2 weeks.

AIOLI

½ cup extra-virgin olive oil

½ cup canola oil

2 cloves garlic

½ teaspoon salt

2 egg yolks

1½ teaspoons Dijon mustard

Grated zest and juice of ½ lemon

Freshly ground black pepper

Makes about 1½ cups

A popular sauce in the south of France, aioli is commonly served with vegetables and seafood but also makes a great spread for burgers, panini, and other sandwiches. Although traditionally it contains only oil, garlic, egg yolks, lemon juice, salt, and pepper, here we have dressed it up with a bit of mustard. You can also flavor it with fresh thyme or oregano, replace the lemon with another citrus such as orange or lime, or substitute a little bit of grated horseradish for the mustard.

Stir together the oils in a measuring cup. Sprinkle ¼ teaspoon of the salt over the garlic and mince, smash, and scrape with the side and edge of the knife until a paste forms.

Transfer the garlic paste to a bowl and whisk in the egg yolks, Dijon mustard, and lemon zest and juice. While whisking constantly, add the oil drop by drop at first, until the mixture begins to thicken, and then in a very slow, steady stream. Continue whisking until the oil is fully incorporated and the mixture is smooth and thickened. Whisk in the remaining ¼ teaspoon of salt and a few twists of pepper.

The sauce will keep in an airtight container in the refrigerator for up to 1 week.

EGG BUTTER

8 hard-boiled eggs
(page 11), peeled
and chopped into
¼-inch pieces

½ cup unsalted butter,
at room temperature

½ teaspoon salt

Freshly ground black
pepper

Makes about 1½ cups

Although this classic Finnish condiment calls for just two ingredients, eggs and butter, plus a little seasoning, it is a deliciously indulgent spread. Slather it on a slice of your favorite bread or a hot piece of toast for a simple but hearty breakfast or snack.

Combine the eggs, butter, salt, and a few twists of pepper in a bowl and, using a fork, mix together until thoroughly combined and spreadable. Taste and adjust the seasoning.

The egg butter will keep in an airtight container for up to 1 week.

HOLLANDAISE SAUCE

4 egg yolks

Juice of ½ lemon

½ cup unsalted butter,
melted, or clarified
butter

½ teaspoon salt

¼ teaspoon freshly
ground black pepper

Pinch of cayenne
pepper

Makes about 1½ cups

One of the most decadent and delicious egg-and-butter-based sauces, hollandaise is surprisingly easy to make at home. The key to success is to add the melted butter very slowly. If you do add it too quickly, the sauce will "break," or separate into liquid and partially solid parts. If your sauce does break, all is not lost. Just whisk in 1 to 2 tablespoons of boiling water, a couple droplets at a time until fully incorporated, and the sauce comes back together.

Whisk together the egg yolks and lemon juice in a heatproof bowl until doubled in volume. Place the bowl over gently simmering water in a saucepan, making sure the bottom of the bowl is not touching the water. While whisking constantly and keeping the water at a gentle simmer, begin drizzling in the butter in a fine, steady stream. Continue to whisk until the butter is fully incorporated and the sauce is smooth and thickened. Whisk in the salt, black pepper, and cayenne pepper, and then taste and adjust the seasoning.

Remove the bowl from over the simmering water and use the sauce immediately, or cover with plastic wrap, pressing it directly against the surface of the sauce until ready to use. This is fine to do if using the sauce within 1 hour of preparation. Otherwise hollandaise will keep in an airtight container in the refrigerator for up to 3 days. Although the sauce can be reheated, it is usually at high risk of "breaking" or "curdling"; for that reason, we suggest making a fresh batch of hollandaise sauce as needed.

BÉARNAISE SAUCE

4 egg yolks

1½ tablespoons tarragon vinegar

½ cup unsalted butter, melted, or clarified butter

1½ tablespoons minced fresh tarragon

½ teaspoon salt

¼ teaspoon freshly ground black pepper

Makes about 1½ cups

Béarnaise sauce is similar to hollandaise sauce, but with the addition of shallots, tarragon vinegar, and fresh tarragon, simmered together before being whisked into the finished sauce. We've simplified our béarnaise sauce by excluding the shallots and adding the vinegar and fresh tarragon directly to the sauce. Because the anise flavor of tarragon is versatile, you'll see béarnaise paired with everything from seared chicken breasts and grilled steaks to seafood and eggs. Most grocery stores carry tarragon vinegar, but it can also be made by immersing a few tarragon sprigs in 1 cup white wine vinegar for at least 3 days.

Whisk together the egg yolks and vinegar in a heatproof bowl until the mixture has doubled in volume. Place the bowl over gently simmering water in asaucepan, making sure the bottom of the bowl is not touching the water. While whisking constantly and keeping the water at a gentle simmer, begin drizzling in the butter in a fine, steady stream. Continue to whisk until the butter is fully incorporated and the sauce is smooth and thick. Whisk in the tarragon, salt, and pepper.

Remove the bowl from over the simmering water and use the sauce immediately, or cover with plastic wrap, pressing it directly against the surface of the sauce until ready to use. This is okay to do if using the sauce within 1 hour of preparation. Although the sauce can be reheated, it is usually at high risk of "breaking" or "curdling"; for that reason, we suggest making a fresh batch of béarnaise sauce as needed.

CRÈME ANGLAISE

1⅓ cups heavy cream

⅔ cup whole milk

⅓ cup plus 2 tablespoons superfine sugar

1 vanilla bean, split lengthwise, or 1½ teaspoons pure vanilla extract

6 egg yolks

Makes about 1½ cups

Creamy yet light, this vanilla-infused custard sauce is perfect spooned over fresh berries, peaches, or other fruits. It is also delicious served over pound or sponge cake and beignets, as they readily soak it up.

Whisk together the cream, milk, and 2 tablespoons of the sugar in a saucepan. If using a vanilla bean, use the tip of a knife to scrape the vanilla seeds from inside each pod half and add the seeds to the pan along with the pod halves. If using vanilla extract, reserve for adding later. Place the pan over medium-low heat and heat until small bubbles begin to form around the edges of the pan and then remove from the heat.

Meanwhile, whisk together the yolks and the remaining ⅓ cup of sugar in a bowl for 2 to 3 minutes, until pale yellow and fluffy. While whisking constantly, pour about ½ cup of the cream mixture into the yolk mixture in a slow, steady stream. Then, while still whisking constantly, gradually pour the cream-yolk mixture into the saucepan.

(continues on the next page)

Return the pan to medium-low heat and cook the sauce, stirring frequently, for 10 to 12 minutes, until the mixture is thick enough to coat the back of a wooden spoon and holds a trail drawn by a fingertip. While the sauce is cooking, prepare an ice-water bath.

Remove the pan from the heat and remove and discard the vanilla pods. Or, if using vanilla extract, stir it into the sauce now. Pour the sauce into a bowl and nest the bowl in the ice-water bath. Let the sauce cool completely, stirring it occasionally and taking care not to slosh any ice water into it.

Cover the cooled sauce with plastic wrap, pressing it directly against the surface, and refrigerate for at least 2 hours before using. The sauce will keep in an airtight container in the refrigerator for up to 5 days.

SABAYON

6 egg yolks

½ cup superfine sugar

⅓ cup plus 2 tablespoons dry white wine

Makes about 1½ cups

Although this light, sweet sauce calls for just three ingredients, you will also need a good measure of stamina to whip it to its classic thick, foamy finish. It makes a great sauce for a variety of desserts, from fruit to cake to cobbler, but it can also be eaten on its own, in a dessert glass with a spoon.

Whisk together the egg yolks, sugar, and wine in a heatproof bowl. Place the bowl over gently simmering water in a saucepan, making sure the bottom of the bowl is not touching the water. While keeping the water at a gentle simmer, whisk the yolk mixture constantly until it is completely foamy and is thick enough to hold its shape when scooped up with the whisk and then allowed to fall back into the bowl. No liquid should be visible at the bottom of the bowl. This can take 6 to 8 minutes. Never stop whisking or you will end up with shreds of scrambled egg. If you tire so much you must stop, be sure to remove the bowl from over the water—but do so only briefly so your mixture doesn't loose aeration and turn flat. Serve the sauce immediately.

PASTA DOUGHS

Fresh pasta is something we find ourselves making more often these days. We generally find it more flavorful than dried pasta and its texture more satisfying. The three doughs that follow are among our favorites. Each of them can be tightly wrapped and refrigerated for up to 2 days. Once a dough is rolled out and cut, it can be cooked right away or, depending on the shape and size of the pasta, it can be twirled into nests, hung over a rod, or spread out on a floured surface and left to dry. When the pasta is fully dried, it can be stored in an airtight container in a cool, dry place for up to 1 month.

Always make sure that you allow the dough to rest, as instructed in each recipe, to give the gluten time to relax. Otherwise, the dough can be difficult to roll out and cut.

BASIC EGG PASTA

1 cup all-purpose flour

¾ cup semolina flour

2 eggs

1½ tablespoons extra-virgin olive oil

Makes about 1 pound

This recipe produces a firm dough that requires some muscle if you are rolling it out by hand. It is especially well suited to cutting into long strands that are then cooked and dressed with a tomato sauce or pesto. We also use it for the ravioli on page 115.

Whisk together the flours in a bowl. Scoop out and set aside ¼ cup of the flour mixture. Mound the remaining flour mixture in the bowl or on a work surface and make a well in the center. Crack the eggs into the well and then pour the oil over the eggs. Using a fork, whisk together the eggs and oil. Then, using the fork, slowly begin to draw the flour into the well, mixing it with the eggs and oil. Continue mixing in the flour until all of it is incorporated and you have a sticky mass. Now begin adding the reserved flour mixture, a little bit at a time, until the dough is firm and no longer sticky to the touch. If the dough seems too dry, add water, 1 teaspoon at a time.

Dust a clean work surface with flour and transfer the dough to the floured surface. Knead the dough until smooth and elastic, 4 to 6 minutes. Wrap the dough in plastic wrap and let rest for about 20 minutes to allow the gluten to relax.

Roll out the dough ¹⁄₁₆ inch thick on a clean floured work surface with a rolling pin. Alternatively, use a pasta machine, following the manufacturer's instructions. Cut as directed in individual recipes or into sheets, strands, or shapes as desired.

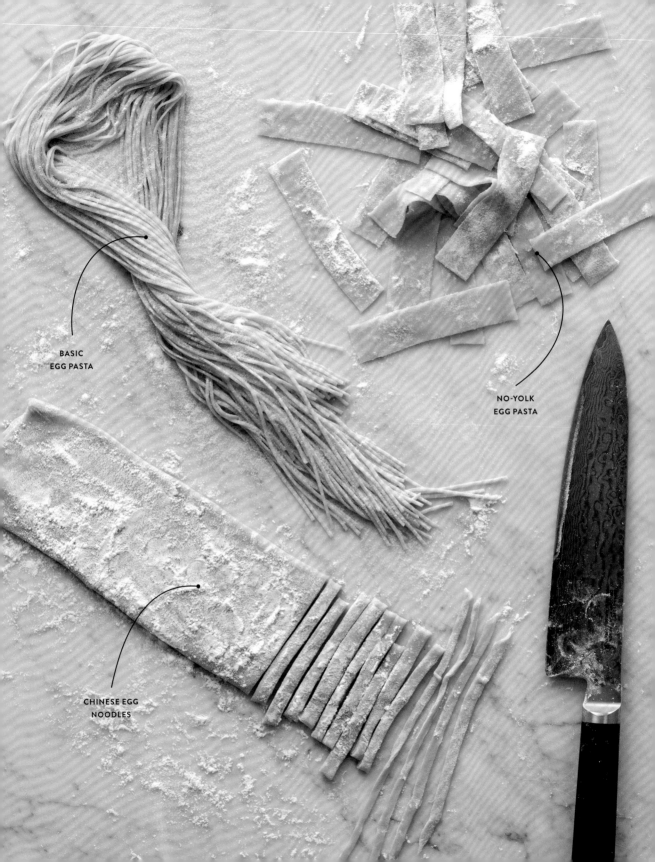

BASIC
EGG PASTA

NO-YOLK
EGG PASTA

CHINESE EGG
NOODLES

CHINESE EGG NOODLES

1½ cups plus 2 tablespoons all-purpose flour

½ teaspoon baking soda

½ teaspoon salt

3 eggs, lightly beaten

2 tablespoons tapioca flour

Makes about 1 pound

Chinese noodles can be prepared in a variety of ways: boiled, panfried, stir-fried, steamed, in soup, or with gravy. We also like to bring them across the border and use them in big, steaming bowls of Japanese ramen. Each of the cooking methods can yield a different result: soft and buttery when boiled or steamed, crisp with a chewy center when panfried, or rich and slippery when coated with gravy.

Whisk together the flour, baking soda, and salt in a bowl. Mound the flour mixture in the bowl, make a well in the center, and add the eggs to the well. Using a fork, slowing begin to draw the flour into the well, mixing it with the eggs. Continue to mixing until all of the flour is incorporated and a dough forms.

Dust a work surface with tapioca flour and turn the dough out onto the floured surface. Knead the dough until soft and elastic, about 5 minutes. Cover the dough with plastic wrap and let rest for about 10 minutes to relax the gluten.

Roll out the dough ⅛ inch thick on a clean floured work surface with a rolling pin. Alternatively, use a pasta machine, following the manufacturer's instructions. Cut into strands of desired width.

NO-YOLK EGG PASTA

1½ cups all-purpose flour

¾ teaspoon salt

2 egg whites

1 tablespoon extra-virgin olive oil

Makes about 1 pound

When we're in the mood for pasta on the lighter side, we turn to this recipe, which calls for egg whites rather than whole eggs or egg yolks. The flavor is milder and the texture is softer than dough made with egg yolks. It's also a good option for anyone looking for a low-cholesterol alternative.

Whisk together the flour and salt in a bowl. Scoop out and set aside ½ cup of the flour mixture. Mound the remaining flour mixture in the bowl or on a work surface and make a well in the center. Drop the whites into the well and then pour the oil over the whites. Using a fork, whisk together the egg whites and oil. Then, using the fork, slowly begin to draw the flour into the well, mixing it with the eggs and oil. Continue mixing in the flour until all of it is incorporated and you have a sticky mass. Now begin adding the reserved flour mixture, a little bit at a time, until the dough is firm and no longer sticky to the touch. If the dough seems too dry, add water, 1 teaspoon at a time.

Dust a clean work surface with flour and transfer the dough to the floured surface. Knead the dough until smooth and elastic, 3 to 5 minutes. Wrap the dough in plastic wrap and let rest for about 20 minutes to allow the gluten to relax.

Roll out the dough 1/16 inch thick on a clean floured work surface with a rolling pin. Alternatively, use a pasta machine, following the manufacturer's instructions. Cut the pasta into ½ by 1½-inch strands.

CHALLAH

BRIOCHE

SOFT PRETZELS

HAWAIIAN SWEET ROLLS

BREADS

One of our favorite things about making bread is the lovely aroma of baking that filters its way through the entire apartment. We also just feel so accomplished after we've tackled baking bread from scratch. We've provided recipes below for some of our favorite egg-based breads. You'll notice we've added soft pretzels to the list. Although soft pretzels are generally made without eggs actually mixed into the dough, we love the added richness it gives to the soft and chewy pretzels, and now it's the only way we're willing to make them at home!

BRIOCHE BUNS

½ cup plus
2 tablespoons whole milk, heated to lukewarm (110°F)

3½ tablespoons superfine sugar

2½ teaspoons active dry yeast

3 eggs, lightly beaten

¾ cup unsalted butter, at room temperature, cut into small cubes

1½ teaspoons salt

4½ cups bread flour

TOPPING

1 egg yolk, lightly beaten with 1½ tablespoons water, for egg wash

3½ tablespoons salted butter, melted

Makes 9 buns

Brioche is wonderfully decadent and one of our favorite breads. We love the shiny crust and the rich and buttery center. We've shaped the dough into hardy buns because they perfectly suit our burgers and sandwiches. But instead you can form the dough into smaller rolls or slider buns.

Stir together the milk and 1½ teaspoons of the sugar in a large bowl. Sprinkle the yeast evenly over the top and let stand for about 10 minutes, until foamy.

Stir the eggs, butter, salt, and the remaining 3 tablespoons of sugar into proofed yeast. The mixture will look chunky. Stir in 4 cups of the flour. ½ cup at a time, continuing to stir until the dough just comes together.

Using the remaining ½ cup of flour, lightly flour a work surface and turn the dough out onto it. Knead the dough (adding more flour as needed to prevent the dough from sticking to the surface) for 8 to 10 minutes, until the dough is smooth, soft, and elastic. Shape the dough into a smooth ball. Lightly oil a large bowl, transfer the dough to it, and turn the ball to coat the surface with oil. Cover the bowl with a damp kitchen towel and let the dough rise at warm room temperature for about 1½ hours, until doubled in size.

Line a baking sheet with parchment paper. Punch down the dough, turn it out onto a lightly floured work surface, and gently reshape it into a ball. Cut the dough into 9 equal pieces, then shape each piece into a ball. Place the balls on the prepared baking sheet, spacing them about 3 inches apart. Cover the pan loosely with plastic wrap and let the dough rise at warm room temperature for about 1 hour, until almost doubled in size.

Preheat the oven to 375°F. Generously brush the top of each bun with the egg wash. Bake for 30 to 35 minutes, until golden brown. Remove from the oven and brush the bun's with the butter. Transfer the buns to a wire rack and let cool for 30 to 60 minutes before serving.

The buns will keep in an airtight container, at room temperature, for up to 3 days.

CHALLAH

1¼ cups lukewarm water (110°F)

4 tablespoons honey, warmed

1½ teaspoons active dry yeast

3 tablespoons unsalted butter, melted

1 egg, lightly beaten

1 egg yolk, lightly beaten

1¼ teaspoons salt

4½ to 5 cups bread flour

TOPPING

1 egg, lightly beaten with 1½ tablespoons water, for egg wash

2 teaspoons poppy seeds (optional)

Makes 1 large loaf or two smaller loaves

One of things we like about making egg-rich challah is how soft and pliable the dough is (similar to brioche dough), which makes it particularly easy to form into the traditional braid shape. It also means that if you fumble when you are braiding, you can undo your mistake and try again.

Stir together the water and 2 tablespoons of the honey in a large bowl. Sprinkle the yeast evenly over the top and let stand for about 5 minutes, until foamy.

Stir the butter, egg, egg yolk, salt, and the remaining 2 tablespoons of honey into the proofed yeast mixture. The mixture will look curdled. Stir in 4½ cups of the flour, ½ cup at a time, continuing to stir until the dough comes together in a rough mass.

Lightly flour a work surface and turn the dough out onto it. Knead the dough (adding more flour as needed to prevent it from sticking to the surface) for 8 to 10 minutes, until the dough is smooth, soft, and elastic. Shape the dough into a smooth ball. Lightly oil a large bowl, transfer the dough to it, and turn the ball to coat the surface with oil. Cover the bowl with a damp kitchen towel and let the dough rise at warm room temperature for about 1½ hours, until doubled in size.

Line a baking sheet with parchment paper. Punch down the dough, turn it out onto a lightly floured work surface, and gently reshape it into a ball. Cut the dough into 3 equal pieces, shape each piece into a ball, and roll each ball into a rope about 30 inches long. Lay the strands side by side on a prepared baking sheet (it's okay if the strands hang over the pan). Pinch the strands together at one end and then braid them, forming a tight braid and tucking under both ends when the braid finished. Cover the baking sheet loosely with plastic wrap and let the dough rise at warm room temperature for about 1 hour, until almost doubled in size.

Preheat the oven to 375°F.

Generously brush the braid with the egg wash and then sprinkle evenly with the poppy seeds. Bake for 32 to 36 minutes, until golden brown.

Transfer the loaf to a wire rack and let cool for at least 1 hour before slicing. Store bread in an airtight container for up to 3 days.

SOFT PRETZELS

1 cup lukewarm
water (110°F)

1 tablespoon
superfine sugar

1 tablespoon active
dry yeast

1 egg

1 teaspoon salt

4¼ cups
bread flour

6 cups water

5½ tablespoons
baking soda

TOPPING

1 egg, lightly beaten
with 1½ tablespoons
water, for egg wash

½ cup black
sesame seeds

½ cup coarse sea salt

Makes 9 pretzels

Pretzel dough does not traditionally call for an egg, but we like the added richness and pleasantly chewy texture it contributes. We have topped these pretzels with coarse sea salt and black sesame seeds, but you can use just the salt or the sesame seeds, or you can substitute a different topping, such as crushed nuts, grated Parmesan, or cinnamon-sugar. You can also bake the pretzels with no topping and then generously brush them with melted salted butter the moment you pull them from the oven.

Stir together the water and sugar in a large bowl. Sprinkle the yeast evenly over the top and let stand for about 5 minutes, until foamy.

Stir the egg and salt into the proofed yeast. Then stir in the flour, 1 cup at a time, continuing to stir until the dough comes together in a rough mass.

Lightly flour a work surface and turn the dough out onto it. Knead the dough (adding more flour as needed to prevent dough from sticking to the surface) for 8 to 10 minutes, until the dough is smooth, soft, and elastic. Shape the dough into a ball.

Line 2 baking sheets with parchment paper. Cut the dough into 9 equal pieces. Working with 1 piece at a time, roll the dough into a rope 22 to 24 inches long, then twist the rope into a classic pretzel shape: form the rope in a U, grasp an end of the rope in each hand, cross the ends over each other twice, creating a small twist, and then bring the ends down to the bottom of the U, to finish the shape. (Or, if you prefer, shape the rope into a figure eight.) As the pretzels are shaped, transfer them to the prepared baking sheets, spacing them 2 inches apart. Cover the pans loosely with plastic wrap and let the dough rise at warm room temperature for about 40 minutes, until almost doubled in size.

Preheat the oven to 400°F.

Combine the water and baking soda in a deep stockpot and bring to a boil over high heat. One at a time, dip the pretzels into the boiling water for about 30 seconds, then carefully return them to the baking sheets.

Generously brush the pretzels with the egg wash and sprinkle with the sesame seeds and sea salt. Using a small, sharp knife, cut a 1-inch-long slash along one side of each pretzel. Bake the pretzels for 16 to 18 minutes, until they are golden brown. Transfer the pretzels to a wire rack and let cool for at least 30 minutes before serving.

The pretzels will keep in an airtight container at room temperature for up to 3 days.

HAWAIIAN SWEET ROLLS

½ cup whole milk, heated to lukewarm (110°F)

½ cup honey, warmed

4 teaspoons active dry yeast

3 eggs, lightly beaten

1 cup pineapple juice

½ cup unsalted butter, melted and cooled

½ teaspoon salt

7½ cups all-purpose flour

1 egg, lightly beaten with 1½ tablespoons water, for egg wash

Makes 24 rolls

Their mild sweetness and soft texture make these rolls irresistible. You can shape the dough into two loaves, but we like baking small rolls, splitting them, and then stuffing them with salty, cured meats and sharp cheeses. Although it may sound odd, we also like to slip a single scoop of ice cream into a split roll. The marriage of melting ice cream and the subtle sweetness of the roll is a perfect union.

Stir together the milk and ¼ cup of the honey in a large bowl. Sprinkle the yeast evenly over the top and let stand for about 5 minutes, until foamy.

Stir the eggs, pineapple juice, butter, salt, and the remaining ¼ cup of honey into the proofed yeast.

Stir in the flour, ½ cup at a time, until the dough comes together in a rough mass.

Lightly flour a work surface and turn the dough out onto it. Knead the dough (adding more flour as needed to prevent the dough from sticking to the surface) for 6 to 8 minutes, until the dough is smooth, soft, and elastic. Shape the dough into a smooth ball. Lightly oil a large bowl, transfer the dough to it, and turn the ball to coat the surface with oil. Cover the bowl with a damp kitchen towel and let the dough rise at warm room temperature for about 1½ hours, until doubled in size.

Oil a 9 by 13-inch pan and an 8-inch square pan. Punch down the dough, turn it out onto a lightly floured surface, and gently reshape it into a ball. Cut the dough into 24 equal pieces, and shape each piece into a ball. Arrange 15 of the balls in the larger pan and the remaining 9 balls in the smaller pan, spacing them about 1½ inches apart. Cover the pans loosely with plastic wrap and let the dough rise at warm room temperature for about 1 hour, until almost doubled in size.

Preheat the oven to 350°F.

Brush the top of each roll with the egg wash. Bake for 25 to 30 minutes, until golden brown. Transfer the rolls to a wire rack and let cool at least 30 minutes before serving.

The rolls will keep in an airtight container at room temperature for 3 to 5 days.

MORNING

MEDITERRANEAN-STYLE BAKED EGG BOATS

6 eggs

⅔ cup sour cream

½ yellow onion, diced

¼ cup diced dry-packed sun-dried tomatoes

5 ounces frozen spinach, thawed, well drained, and chopped

4 ounces feta cheese, crumbled

1½ teaspoons salt

½ teaspoon freshly ground black pepper

4 square ciabatta rolls

These baked egg boats were born out of our dual love for baked eggs and for soup served in a bread bowl. Why not combine the two concepts and bake a savory quiche in a hollowed-out baguette? Serve these boats for a terrific breakfast or pack one up for a midafternoon snack-on-the-go. If you cannot find square ciabatta rolls, mini baguettes—sourdough or French—will work, too.

Preheat the oven to 375°F. Line a baking sheet with parchment paper.

Whisk together the eggs, sour cream, onion, tomatoes, spinach, feta, salt, and pepper in a bowl, mixing well. Cut off the top ½ inch or so of each ciabatta roll, leaving a ½-¾-inch perimeter around the top, then pull out most of the doughy insides. Place the rolls, hollow side up, on the prepared baking sheet. Divide the egg mixture evenly among the hollowed-out rolls.

Bake for 25 to 30 minutes, until the filling is set in the center and golden brown. Let cool for about 5 minutes before serving. Cut each boat crosswise into strips to serve.

AREPA DE HUEVO

2½ cups hot water

2 cups masarepa*

3 tablespoons vegetable oil, plus more for brushing and frying

¾ teaspoon salt

10 medium eggs

Salt and freshly ground black pepper

To make arepas, you will need the precooked white cornmeal most commonly known as masarepa and sometimes labeled "arepa flour," "masa de arepa," "masa al instante," or "harina precocida." P.A.N., a popular brand, can be found in some Latin American markets and online. Do not confuse masarepa with the more widely available masa harina.

Our first experience with arepas was at Caracas Arepa Bar, a Venezuelan restaurant in New York City. We were hot, sweaty, and exhausted from walking the city streets all day. The wait for a table was over an hour, but the arepas were well worth the time, and we have obsessed over the little pockets of crispy dough filled with shredded meat ever since. In our Colombian-inspired version, we drop a raw egg into the pocket, then fry it up for a compact, handheld breakfast treat that's great on the go. We dress the pockets with our favorite hot sauces—perfect for cutting the richness and adding some kick!

Stir together the water, masarepa, oil, and salt in a large bowl just until the mixture comes together. Cover with a damp kitchen towel and let rest for 15 to 20 minutes. After the dough has rested, work out any lumps in the dough with your hands.

Preheat the oven to 200°F. Line two baking sheets with parchment paper and a third baking sheet with paper towels.

Pinch off about 5 tablespoons of the dough and pat it between your palms into an even, flat disk about 4 inches in diameter and ½ inch thick. Lightly brush both sides of the disk with oil and place the disk on a parchment-lined baking sheet. Repeat with the remaining dough, shaping 10 disks total and placing all of the disks on the same baking sheet.

Set a cast-iron or other heavy skillet over medium-high heat and lightly brush the skillet with oil. When the skillet is hot, arrange as many disks in it as will fit without crowding and cook, turning once, for 7 to 10 minutes on each side, until the arepas are golden brown on both sides and make a hollow sound when picked up and tapped. If the arepas seem to be cooking too quickly, lower the heat to medium. As the arepas are ready, transfer them to the second parchment-lined baking sheet and keep warm in the oven. Repeat with the remaining disks.

Pour the oil into a deep pot to a depth of 3 inches and heat to 350°F.

Make a 1½-inch slit around the edge of each arepa, with a paring knife, to create a pocket. Crack an egg into a ramekin or small bowl and carefully slip it into an arepa pocket. Holding the arepa cut side up, carefully lower it into the oil and cook for 3 to 5 minutes, until the arepa is lightly golden and the egg is fully cooked. Transfer the arepa to the towel-lined baking sheet to drain. Season with salt and pepper. Repeat with the remaining arepas and eggs. Serve hot.

TIP: Keep the finished arepas warm on a baking sheet in an oven set to 200°F while frying the remaining arepas, until you're ready to serve them.

BLACKBERRY-STUFFED CROISSANT FRENCH TOAST

FILLING

¾ cup (about 4 ounces) fresh blackberries, plus more for garnish

2½ tablespoons superfine sugar

Grated zest and juice of ½ lemon

6 ounces cream cheese, at room temperature

½ teaspoon ground cinnamon

TOAST

4 plain croissants

4 eggs

2 egg yolks

½ cup buttermilk

½ cup heavy cream

⅓ cup firmly packed light brown sugar

1½ teaspoons pure vanilla extract

½ teaspoon ground cinnamon

¼ teaspoon ground cardamom

Pinch of salt

6 tablespoons unsalted butter

Confectioners' sugar, maple syrup, or honey, for serving

I ate French toast only a handful of times growing up, and it wasn't the typical sweet breakfast—dusted with confectioners' sugar or drizzled with sticky maple syrup—in my house. My mom, though a total pro with Korean foods, occasionally attempted hilarious, though endearing riffs on classic American dishes. My childhood French toast was a slice of bread cloaked in the thinnest egg omelet and served with ketchup. However, to say I didn't happily gobble it up every time it was set in front of me would be a lie. But this version of French toast, made with flaky croissants, properly sweetened, and stuffed with decadent blackberry compote and cream cheese, is our dream version. We call it the dessert of breakfasts! - Jenny

To make the filling, combine the berries, sugar, and lemon zest and juice in a small saucepan over medium-low heat and cook, stirring occasionally for 10 to 12 minutes until the berries have softened and are juicy. Gently mash the berries with the back of a spoon and continue to simmer for 5 to 7 minutes longer until the mixture thickens slightly. Remove from the heat and let cool completely. When the mixture is cool, fold in the cream cheese and cinnamon.

To make the French toast, split each croissant in half horizontally and spread each bottom half with about 3 tablespoons of the berry filling. Replace the top halves and press gently until securely closed.

In a large, shallow bowl, whisk together the eggs, egg yolks, buttermilk, cream, brown sugar, vanilla, cinnamon, cardamom, and salt. Soak the filled croissants in the egg mixture for 5 minutes and then flip and soak for 5 minutes longer.

Melt 3 tablespoons of the butter in a cast-iron or other heavy skillet over medium heat. When the butter is hot, place 2 stuffed croissants in the skillet and cook, turning once, 4 to 5 minutes on each side, until golden brown and lightly crisp. Transfer to a plate and keep warm. Repeat with the remaining 3 tablespoons of butter and 2 stuffed croissants.

To serve, place each croissant on a plate and dust with confectioners' sugar or drizzle with maple syrup or honey. Serve immediately.

EGG BHURJI

2 tablespoons ghee or unsalted butter

½ yellow onion, diced

1 Roma tomato, seeded and diced

2 cloves garlic, minced

1 serrano chile, seeded and diced

½ teaspoon peeled and minced fresh ginger

2 teaspoons tomato paste

¼ teaspoon ground coriander

¼ teaspoon garam masala

¼ teaspoon ground turmeric

Pinch of smoked paprika

2 tablespoons minced fresh cilantro

7 eggs, lightly beaten

Salt and freshly ground black pepper

Scrambled eggs are a classic American breakfast dish, but there are many flavor-packed versions worldwide that we also like. We both adore the bright flavors of India and this Indian take on scrambled eggs. The bold spices are addictive and are perfectly complemented by a finish of fragrant cilantro. Serve the eggs with grilled naan for a hearty breakfast.

Melt the ghee in a large skillet over medium-high heat. Add the onion and sauté for about 5 minutes, until translucent. Add the tomato, garlic, chile, and ginger and sauté for 1 minute longer. Stir in the tomato paste, coriander, garam masala, turmeric, paprika, and 1½ tablespoons of the cilantro, and then lower the heat to medium. Gradually add the eggs while stirring to mix with the seasoning; and then cook, stirring gently, until the eggs are cooked hard.

Divide the eggs among four plates, season lightly with salt and pepper, and top with the remaining 1½ teaspoons cilantro. Serve immediately.

EGG CLOUDS

8 eggs

1 tablespoon grated
Parmesan cheese

½ teaspoon salt

Freshly ground black
pepper

This simple dish is as delicious to eat as it is appealing to look at, with whole creamy yolks and a cloud of egg whites baked to perfection. For an even more flavorful treat, add one or more of your favorite ingredients to the beaten whites before baking. We've enjoyed mixing in crumbled cooked breakfast sausage or bacon, or sautéed diced yellow onion and bell pepper seasoned with minced fresh herbs.

Preheat the oven to 375°F. Line a baking sheet with parchment paper.

Separate the eggs, being careful to keep the egg yolks whole. Put the egg whites in a clean bowl and beat with a stand mixer or handheld mixer on medium-high speed until medium-stiff peaks form that hold their shape when the beater is lifted but are not at all dry. Using a rubber spatula, gently fold in the Parmesan and salt in a few quick strokes, taking care not to deflate the whites.

Scoop the egg white mixture onto the prepared baking sheet in 8 mounds, using ½ to ¾ cup for each mound and spacing the mounds at least 1 inch apart. Using the back of a spoon, create a small well in the center of each mound. Carefully place an egg yolk in each well.

For creamy yolks, bake for 14 to 16 minutes, until the yolks have set and the whites are light golden brown. For runny yolks, remove from the oven after 8 to 10 minutes.

Season with salt and pepper and serve hot.

HUEVOS RANCHEROS

TOMATO SALSA

⅓ cup canned tomato sauce

½ teaspoon white wine vinegar

Pinch of superfine sugar

4 Roma tomatoes, seeded and diced

½ small yellow onion, diced

1 clove garlic, minced

2 tablespoons minced fresh cilantro

Juice of 1 lime

Salt and freshly ground black pepper

EGGS

Canola oil, for frying

4 (4- to 5-inch) corn tortillas

2 cups cooked black beans, heated

4 eggs

4 tablespoons unsalted butter

¼ cup crumbled Cotija cheese, for garnish

2 tablespoons minced fresh cilantro, for garnish

4 lime wedges, for serving

Hot sauce, for serving

A plate of huevos rancheros, or "ranch-style eggs," is typically fried eggs sitting on a couple of corn tortillas, topped with a chile-laced tomato sauce, and accompanied with refried beans, rice, and guacamole. In our version, we keep the fried eggs and corn tortillas, but we use black beans in place of the usual pintos, top our homemade salsa with a little crumbled cheese, and skip the guacamole and rice. When you pop open the runny egg yolk, it mingles with the other ingredients on the plate to create a rich and satisfying marriage of flavors.

To make the salsa, combine the tomato sauce, vinegar, and sugar in a small saucepan over medium heat, bring to a simmer, and simmer for 5 minutes. Remove from the heat and let cool.

Combine the diced tomatoes, onion, garlic, cilantro, and lime juice in a bowl and toss to mix well. Add the cooled tomato sauce, stir to mix evenly, and season with salt and pepper. Set the salsa aside.

Heat 1 inch of oil in a nonstick skillet over medium-high heat. When the oil is hot, add 1 tortilla and fry for about 2 minutes on each side, or until golden brown and crisp. Drain onto paper towels and lightly season with salt. Repeat with the remaining tortillas, adding more oil to the pan if needed and putting each on a plate. Spoon ½ cup black beans over each tortilla and set the plates in a warm spot.

Wipe out the skillet and return it to medium heat. Following the directions for fried eggs (page 12) fry 2 eggs at a time in butter over easy, over medium, or over hard, as desired, then transfer each egg to a plate, placing it atop the beans. Repeat with the remaining 2 eggs.

To serve, top each egg with some salsa and a sprinkling of cheese. Garnish with the cilantro and pass the lime wedges and hot sauce at the table.

KHAI YAT SAI

FILLING

3½ tablespoons vegetable oil

1 pound ground pork

1 tablespoon oyster sauce

1 teaspoon fish sauce

1 small yellow onion, diced

2 cloves garlic, minced

2 teaspoons minced fresh lemongrass

½ teaspoon peeled and minced fresh ginger

½ serrano chile, seeded and minced

⅓ cup frozen petite green peas, thawed

1 green onion, white and green parts, thinly sliced

¼ teaspoon salt

¼ teaspoon freshly ground black pepper

OMELETS

6 eggs

1 red jalapeño chile, seeded and minced

2 green onions, white and green parts, thinly sliced

4 tablespoons vegetable oil

Salt and freshly ground black pepper

Many countries have a popular filled omelet in their cuisine. This Thai version, stuffed with ground pork, is one of our favorites because its thin, crepe-style omelet allows the bold, savory filling to take center stage. Although it appears here in the breakfast chapter, it also makes a quick and easy dinner. Either time of day, don't hold back on the Sriracha sauce!

To make the filling, place a large skillet over medium-high heat and add 2 tablespoons of the oil. When the oil is hot, add the pork and cook, breaking it up with a wooden spoon, for about 4 minutes until about half-cooked. Remove from the heat and transfer the pork to a bowl. Add the oyster sauce and fish sauce, mix well, and set aside.

Wipe out the skillet, return it to medium-high heat, and add the remaining 1½ tablespoons of oil. When the oil is hot, add the yellow onion, garlic, lemongrass, ginger, and serrano chile and sauté, stirring frequently, for 4 to 5 minutes. Return the pork to the skillet, lower the heat to medium, and continue to cook and stir for about 5 minutes, until the pork is cooked through. Gently mix in the peas, green onion, salt, and pepper and remove from the heat. Taste and adjust the seasoning.

To make the omelets, whisk together the eggs, jalapeño chile, and green onion in a bowl. Place an 8-inch skillet over medium heat and add 2 tablespoons of the oil. When the oil is hot, pour a quarter of the egg mixture into the skillet and immediately swirl the pan to form a thin omelet. Lower the heat to medium-low and cook for 3 to 4 minutes, just until the surface sets. Spoon a quarter of the filling over half of the omelet, then gently fold the uncovered half over the filling. Transfer the omelet to a plate and keep warm. Repeat to make three more omelets, adding more oil to the skillet as needed.

Lightly season the omelets with salt and pepper and serve immediately.

QUICHE

CRUST

1¼ cups all-purpose flour

½ teaspoon superfine sugar

½ teaspoon salt

½ cup cold unsalted butter, cut into small cubes

2 tablespoons ice water

1 teaspoon cider vinegar

FILLING

1 tablespoon unsalted butter

½ yellow onion, thinly sliced

3 duck eggs or 5 chicken eggs, lightly beaten

1 cup heavy cream

½ cup shredded Swiss cheese

½ teaspoon salt

¼ teaspoon freshly ground black pepper

Urth Caffé, which is near our office in Los Angeles, serves a perfectly crafted quiche: crust that stays crisp, clear to the bottom, filled with layered toppings suspended in a tender egg custard. Quiche is versatile. In other words, you can easily add nearly anything to it, so it is easy to personalize. Here is our method for a perfect classic quiche, along with eight of our favorite variations.

To make the crust, whisk together the flour, sugar, and salt in a bowl. Scatter the butter over the flour mixture. Then, using two knives or a pastry blender, cut in the butter until the mixture resembles a coarse meal. Stir together the water and vinegar in a small bowl, drizzle over the flour-butter mixture, and toss with a fork until the mixture is evenly moistened and the dough comes together in a rough mass.

Place a large piece of plastic wrap on a work surface and turn out the dough onto the plastic wrap. Using your hands, shape the dough into a flat, thick disk and then wrap the disk in the plastic wrap. Refrigerate for at least 30 minutes.

Have ready a 9 by 1-inch round fluted tart pan. Dust a work surface with a small amount of flour. Unwrap the dough disk, place on the floured surface, and roll out the dough into a round 12 inches in diameter and ⅛ inch thick. Gently drape the dough over the rolling pin, position the pin over the tart pan, and then unroll the dough and center it in the pan. Press the dough evenly onto the bottom and sides of the pan, and then run the pin across the rim of the pan to trim away the excess dough. Using a fork, prick the bottom all over at ½-inch intervals. Refrigerate for 30 minutes.

At least 15 minutes before baking, preheat the oven to 375°F.

Line the crust with aluminum foil and fill with pie weights or dried beans. Bake for 10 to 15 minutes, until the crust becomes pale and slightly translucent. Remove from the oven and then remove the weights and foil and set the crust aside on a wire rack to cool. Leave the oven on.

To make the filling, melt the butter in a skillet over medium heat. Add the onion and sauté for 3 to 5 minutes, until slightly translucent and the edges begin to caramelize. Remove from the heat and let cool. Whisk together the eggs, cream, ¼ cup of the cheese, the salt, and the pepper in a bowl, mixing well. Scatter the onion evenly over the bottom of the crust and then slowly pour in the egg mixture. Sprinkle the remaining ¼ cup of cheese evenly over the top.

Bake for 25 to 30 minutes, until the filling is set and the top is golden brown. Let cool for 5 to 8 minutes before serving.

THREE MEAT

SPINACH & FETA

SUN-DRIED TOMATO
& ARTICHOKE

LORRAINE

CARAMELIZED LEEK &
SWISS

CLASSIC

WILD MUSHROOM &
SMOKED GOUDA

PRIMAVERA

ALL WHITES

VARIATIONS:

THREE MEAT: Replace the Swiss cheese with white Cheddar cheese. Whisk 1 cup of crumbled cooked bacon into the filling. Sprinkle ½ cup of crumbled cooked breakfast sausage and ½ cup of cubed smoked ham over the bottom of the cooled crust before adding the filling.

SPINACH & FETA: Add ½ cup of crumbled feta cheese, 2 teaspoons of minced fresh oregano, 1 teaspoon of minced fresh thyme, and 1 cup of well-drained chopped, cooked spinach to the filling.

SUN-DRIED TOMATO & ARTICHOKE: Add 1 cup of thinly sliced sun-dried tomatoes, 1 cup of quartered marinated artichoke hearts, ½ cup pitted and chopped olives (of your choice), and 1 tablespoon of minced fresh oregano to the filling.

CARAMELIZED LEEK & SWISS: Omit the onion. Thinly slice 4 leeks and sauté in oil for about 15 minutes until caramelized. Let the leeks cool. Mix half of the leeks into the filling and scatter the remaining leeks over the bottom of the crust before adding the filling.

LORRAINE: Add ½ cup of crumbled cooked bacon to the filling. Sprinkle another ½ cup crumbled cooked bacon over the bottom of the cooled crust before adding the filling.

WILD MUSHROOM & SMOKED GOUDA: Replace the Swiss cheese with shredded smoked Gouda cheese. Add ½ cup of sautéed wild mushrooms and 1 tablespoon of minced fresh thyme to the filling. Sprinkle ½ cup of sautéed wild mushrooms over the bottom of the cooled crust before adding the filling.

PRIMAVERA: Add ½ cup of halved cherry tomatoes and 1½ cup of chopped broccoli florets to the filling.

ALL WHITES: Omit the yolks and add 2 additional duck egg whites or 3 additional chicken egg whites. Replace the Swiss cheese with shredded mozzarella.

GYERAN BBANG

1 cup all-purpose flour

1 tablespoon superfine sugar

¼ teaspoon baking powder

¼ teaspoon salt

⅔ cup whole milk

½ teaspoon pure vanilla extract

9 eggs

Salt and freshly ground black pepper

On my most recent visit to Seoul, my cousin and I hit the streets to shop, by which I mean, we ran around the city eating. I was lucky to have him with me, as he had been in South Korea enough times to gain fluency in the country's second language, "Seoul subway." We explored the food all over town, dining in many restaurants, but what really stood out for me was the street food—those rich, greasy fried foods my healthy Korean mom rarely, if ever, cooked at home. Among the most memorable bites was gyeran bbang, a simple pancake-wrapped egg sandwich fried in a skillet. The play of the sweet, crispy pancake against the rich, savory egg was mesmerizing. We bake our version in a pan with the egg on top for better distribution. And we've left our yolks runny because we love a runny yolk! - Jenny

Preheat the oven to 375°F. Lightly oil 8 mini loaf pans (1½ by 3 inches) and arrange on a large baking sheet, or lightly oil 8 wells of a standard muffin pan.

Whisk together the flour, sugar, baking powder, and salt in a bowl. In a separate bowl, whisk together the milk, vanilla, and 1 egg. Gradually whisk the milk mixture into the flour mixture until smooth.

Divide the batter evenly among the prepared loaf pans or muffin wells, filling them each about one-third full. Bake for 8 minutes and then remove from the oven. Crack 1 egg into a small bowl and carefully slip it into a loaf pan or muffin well. Repeat with the remaining 7 eggs. Return the pan(s) to the oven and continue to bake for 5 to 6 minutes, until the egg whites are opaque and the yolks are still runny. For a firmer yolk, bake for an additional 2 to 3 minutes.

Let the "sandwiches" cool for 5 minutes in the loaf pans or muffin wells and then run a thin-bladed knife around the inside of each pan or muffin well to release the sides. Using a small offset spatula, lift each of the gyeran bbang from the pan. Season with salt and pepper and serve warm.

PEPPERED PASTRAMI EGGS BENEDICT

1½ cups hollandaise sauce (page 16)

4 medium eggs

1 teaspoon white wine vinegar or cider vinegar

2 English muffins, split and toasted

8 ounces peppered pastrami, thinly sliced and briefly seared

1 teaspoon chopped thyme

Freshly ground black pepper

I credit eggs Benedict with helping me to graduate from college, as it was my go-to hangover dish. I sing its praises not only because it got me through many a morning class but also for its total lack of shame: a buttered English muffin topped with salty thick-cut ham and two runny poached eggs, all smothered with rich and decadent hollandaise—the more the better. It just screams, "Bring on the heart attack!" This is our almost-classic, no-fuss version, glorious in its own right. - Jenny

Make the hollandaise as directed and keep warm. Poach the eggs with vinegar as directed on page 12.

To assemble each serving, place 2 muffin halves, cut side up and side by side, on a plate. Top each muffin half with a quarter of the pastrami, and then top the pastrami with a poached egg. Generously spoon the hollandaise over each egg, sprinkle with thyme, grind a little pepper over the top, and serve at once.

TIP: If the hollandaise becomes too thick before serving, stir in about 2 tablespoons of warm chicken stock or water to return it to the desired consistency.

KAYA TOAST

KAYA

1 cup full-fat canned coconut milk

1 cup superfine sugar

Pinch of salt

6 or 7 fresh or frozen pandan leaves, each tied into a knot, or ½ teaspoon pandan essence

6 egg yolks, at room temperature

TOAST

4 eggs

4 thick slices French bread, toasted and crusts removed

4 tablespoons salted butter, at room temperature

2 tablespoons tamari

½ cup loosely packed baby arugula

I first encountered this tasty toast at Susan Feniger's former Los Angeles restaurant, Street, where much buzz surrounded the unusual combination of a tamari-seasoned egg sandwiched between thick bread slices spread with kaya, a sweet Southeast Asian coconut jam. The surprisingly harmonious result makes a unique breakfast or an unforgettable appetizer when cut into small pieces. Be sure the egg yolks are at room temperature for the best consistency. Tropical pandan leaves add a nutty-floral flavor to many Southeast Asian dishes. Look for the leaves fresh or frozen or for pandan essence in Asian markets or online. - Teri

To make the kaya, whisk together the coconut milk, ¾ cup of the sugar, and the salt until well blended. Transfer the mixture to a saucepan, add the pandan leaves or pandan essence, and bring to a simmer over medium heat, stirring to dissolve the sugar.

Meanwhile, whisk the egg yolks until pale and creamy. Add the remaining ¼ cup of sugar and whisk until thoroughly incorporated. While whisking constantly, add ¼ cup of the simmering coconut milk mixture to the egg mixture. Return the egg yolk–coconut milk mixture to the saucepan and continue to simmer, whisking constantly for 10 to 12 minutes, until the kaya is thick enough to coat the back of a wooden spoon. Remove from the heat and let cool.

Remove and discard the pandan leaves from the cooled kaya. Transfer to a blender or food processor and process until completely smooth.

Fry the eggs in butter as directed on page 12 and keep warm.

To assemble the toasts, cut each slice of toasted bread in half. Spread each half thinly on one side with the kaya and then spread 1½ teaspoons butter over the kaya on each piece. Sandwich the spread-side halves together to make four half sandwiches. Top each half sandwich with a fried egg, sprinkle the egg with 1½ teaspoons tamari, and top with a quarter of the arugula. Serve at once.

FRITTATA

6 eggs

½ cup shredded mild
Cheddar cheese

2 tablespoons grated
Parmesan cheese

1 teaspoon salt

½ teaspoon freshly
ground black pepper

2 tablespoons unsalted
butter

When we want to impress our brunch guests but time is short, the frittata
comes to the rescue. It is easy to throw together and can be adapted
to nearly any ingredient, fresh or left over, that you have on hand. Eight
of our favorite variations follow the classic recipe. Check them out and
then come up with your own!

Preheat the broiler.

Whisk the eggs in a bowl to break them up and, then whisk in the cheeses, salt,
and pepper.

Place an 8-inch cast-iron or broiler-proof nonstick skillet over medium heat. Add
the butter to the hot pan and swirl the pan to coat the bottom evenly with the
butter. Pour in the egg mixture and stir gently with a rubber spatula. Once the
bottom begins to set, continue to cook without stirring for 3 to 4 minutes, until
the edges begin to set but the center is still runny.

Transfer the skillet to the broiler and broil for 3 to 4 minutes, until the frittata is
set and the top begins to brown lightly.

Use an oven mitt to transfer the hot pan to a heat-safe surface. Let stand for 6 to
8 minutes, then carefully slide frittata onto a cutting board. Cut into 6 wedges,
season with salt and pepper, and serve.

VARIATIONS:

FIVE HERB: Replace the Cheddar
cheese with shredded Fontina cheese
and add 1 teaspoon minced fresh thyme,
1 teaspoon thinly sliced fresh chives,
1 teaspoon minced fresh oregano,
½ teaspoon minced fresh rosemary,
and ½ teaspoon minced fresh sage to
the egg mixture.

WILD MUSHROOM & GOAT CHEESE:
Replace the Cheddar cheese with ⅔ cup
crumbled fresh goat cheese. Omit butter
and sauté 1½ cups wild mushrooms in
2 tablespoons canola oil in the skillet for
about 5 minutes, until softened, before
pouring in the egg mixture.

PANCETTA & CARAMELIZED ONION:
Replace the Cheddar cheese with
shredded Comté or Gruyère cheese
and increase the black pepper to
¾ teaspoon. Scatter 1 cup cooked
diced pancetta and 1 cup caramelized
thinly sliced yellow onion (about
2 onions) over the bottom of the skillet
before pouring in the egg mixture.

OLIVE & SUN-DRIED TOMATO: Replace
the Cheddar cheese with ⅔ cup crumbled
fresh goat cheese. Sprinkle 1 cup chopped
olives (whatever type you like) and ½ cup
chopped dry-packed sun-dried tomatoes
into the skillet before pouring in the egg
mixture.

SMOKED SALMON & DILL

FIVE HERB

SPINACH & FETA

WILD MUSHROOM & GOAT CHEESE

O'BRIEN STYLE

PANCETTA & CARAMELIZED ONION

SAUSAGE, FENNEL & ARUGULA

CLASSIC

OLIVE & SUN-DRIED TOMATO

SAUSAGE, FENNEL & ARUGULA: Replace the Cheddar cheese with shredded Gruyère cheese. Sprinkle 1 cup crumbled cooked breakfast sausage, 1 cup loosely packed baby arugula, and 1 small bulb fennel, trimmed, thinly sliced, and lightly sautéed, over the bottom of the skillet before pouring in the egg mixture.

O'BRIEN STYLE: Dice 2 red potatoes, ½ yellow onion, ½ red bell pepper, and ½ green bell pepper. Sauté the diced vegetables with 2 cloves garlic, minced, in about 3 tablespoons canola oil in the skillet for about 8 minutes, until softened, before pouring in the egg mixture.

SPINACH & FETA: Replace the Cheddar cheese with ⅔ cup crumbled feta cheese. Omit butter and dice ½ of a yellow onion and sauté with 2 cloves garlic, minced, in 1½ tablespoons of canola oil in the skillet for about 5 minutes, until softened. Add 1½ cups wilted spinach (squeezed as dry as possible) and stir to mix before pouring in the egg mixture.

SMOKED SALMON & DILL: Replace the Cheddar cheese with ½ cup sour cream and whisk 1 tablespoon minced fresh dill into the egg mixture. Sprinkle 5 ounces sliced cold-smoked salmon and 3 tablespoons drained capers over the bottom of the skillet before pouring in the egg mixture.

MINI TOAD-IN-A-HOLE SANDWICHES

8 large slices prosciutto

8 slices sourdough
bread, each about
4 inches long and
6 inches wide

½ cup unsalted butter,
at room temperature

8 quail eggs*

8 Campanelli or Roma
tomato slices, each ¼
inch thick

8 large fresh basil leaves

Salt and freshly ground
black pepper

*You can use chicken
eggs instead of quail
eggs. If you opt for that
change, you'll need to
use a whole slice of
bread for each egg and
a 2-inch round cutter.
Also use Roma, rather
than Campanelli,
tomato slices and more
prosciutto and basil
for each sandwich. You
will need to cook the
eggs for 7 to 10 minutes
in the oven, to allow
the whites to set. The
sandwiches won't be
mini bites, either.
Instead, they will be a
fairly substantial meal.

In college, I would make the short trek from Los Angeles to Palm Springs to join my uncle, his family, and my grandparents for Thanksgiving. After stuffing ourselves with turkey and fixings, we would turn in early. In the morning, we would awaken to my cousin Will, busy in the kitchen, proudly making his version of toad in a hole for everyone. Because my ideal breakfast consists of eggs over easy on toast, this new twist on that classic was intriguing. In fact, now I prefer it for the way the toast soaks up a bit of the egg while cooking. We make ours with quail eggs, sandwiched with prosciutto, tomatoes, and fresh basil. - Teri

Preheat the oven to 350°F. Arrange the prosciutto slices in a single layer on a baking sheet and bake for 6 to 8 minutes, until shriveled and crispy. Set the prosciutto aside and raise the oven temperature to 375°F.

Using a 3-inch round cutter, cut 2 rounds from each bread slice. Using a 1-inch round cutter, cut a round from the center of 8 of the bread rounds. Spread all 16 large bread rounds on both sides with the butter. (Discard the small centers and other bread scraps or save for another use.)

Heat a large, ovenproof skillet over medium-high heat. Place the 8 bread rounds without holes in the skillet and toast, turning once, for about 3 minutes on each side, until lightly browned. Divide the toasted bread rounds among 4 plates, placing 2 rounds on each plate. Top each round with a piece of prosciutto, a tomato slice, and a basil leaf. Set aside.

Place the bread rounds with the holes in the center in the skillet and lower the heat to medium. Toast the underside for about 3 minutes, until light brown. Flip the bread rounds and crack 1 egg into the hole of each round. Transfer the skillet to the oven and bake for 3 to 5 minutes, until the whites are opaque and the yolks are still runny.

Place the egg-filled rounds on top of the prepared toast rounds. Season with salt and pepper and serve immediately.

TIP: If you don't have round cutters, use the rim of a 3-inch glass jar or drinking glass as a template to cut the bread rounds and a 1-inch bottle lid to cut the centers.

HAVARTI-DILL POPOVERS

3 tablespoons
unsalted butter,
melted and cooled

¼ cup shredded Havarti
cheese

1 tablespoon minced
fresh dill

2 eggs

1 cup whole milk

½ teaspoon salt

1 cup all-purpose flour

Popovers intimidate most people. They rise up. They collapse. It's stressful. We understand. These popovers will hold their shape for quite a while before collapsing, and even after they do, they will taste every bit as custardy and delicious as the moment you pulled them from the oven. Havarti and dill are our choice for making them special, but feel free to put your own signature on them by substituting your favorite combination of cheese and herbs. To bake the popovers in a standard muffin pan instead of a popover pan, butter and fill 8 muffin wells and reduce the baking time by 3 to 5 minutes, both before and after lowering the temperature.

Preheat the oven to 450°F. Brush a 6-cup popover pan with 1 tablespoon of the butter.

Toss together the cheese and dill in a small bowl and set aside. Whisk together the eggs, milk, the remaining 2 tablespoons of butter, and the salt in a bowl, mixing well. Stir in the flour until only a few lumps remain.

Set aside 6 tablespoons of the batter. Divide the remaining batter evenly among the prepared popover cups, filling them each half full. Sprinkle the cheese-dill mixture evenly over the batter in each cup, using about 2 teaspoons for each cup. Spoon 1 tablespoon of the reserved batter over the cheese mixture in each cup.

Bake for 20 minutes, then lower the temperature to 350°F and continue baking for about 15 minutes longer, until the popovers are puffed and golden brown.

Let the popovers rest in the pan for about 5 minutes before unmolding. Serve warm.

BUTTERMILK PANCAKES

1 cup all-purpose flour

1½ tablespoons superfine sugar

1 teaspoon baking powder

½ teaspoon baking soda

½ teaspoon salt

1 egg, lightly beaten

1 cup buttermilk

2 tablespoons unsalted butter, melted and cooled, plus 4 tablespoons

½ teaspoon pure vanilla extract

Unsalted butter and maple syrup, for serving

I learned my pancake skills on Sunday mornings, watching my dad make flapjacks on a griddle. Although how he knew when it was time to flip was common knowledge (watch for bubbles to form around the edges), my nine-year-old self saw him as a culinary genius. Nowadays I use pancakes as a medium for experimentation, adding ingredients and trying out various flavor combinations. Here is the classic formula, along with plenty of variations to stimulate your own creativity. - Teri

Whisk together the flour, sugar, baking powder, baking soda, and salt in a bowl, mixing well. Stir in the egg, buttermilk, 2 tablespoons of melted butter, and vanilla just until the ingredients are evenly distributed but the batter is still lumpy. Do not overmix.

Place a large griddle or skillet over medium heat, add 1½ teaspoons of the butter, and when the butter melts, swirl the pan to cover the bottom evenly. Making 3 to 4 at a time, ladle ¼ cup of the batter into the skillet and cook for 4 to 5 minutes, until bubbles form on the top of the pancake. Carefully flip the pancake over and continue to cook for 3 to 4 minutes, until cooked through. Transfer the pancake to a serving platter. Cook the remaining batter in the same manner, adding butter to the pan as needed.

Serve warm with butter and maple syrup.

TIP: To make multiple batches, preheat the oven to 200°F and transfer the finished pancakes to a parchment-lined baking sheet in the oven to keep warm while you cook the rest of the batter.

(continues on the next page)

VARIATIONS:

RASPBERRY & RICOTTA: Reduce the buttermilk to ½ cup and add ¾ cup whole milk ricotta cheese. Toss 1 cup fresh raspberries with the juice of ½ lemon and 1 tablespoon all-purpose flour. Gently fold the raspberries into the batter, just until incorporated.

CARROT CAKE: Whisk 1 teaspoon ground cinnamon, ¼ teaspoon freshly grated nutmeg, and ¼ teaspoon ground allspice into the flour mixture. Fold 1 cup shredded, peeled carrot and ½ cup dried currants into the batter just until incorporated. Make cream cheese frosting by whisking together 3½ tablespoons whole milk; 2 tablespoons cream cheese, at room temperature; and ½ teaspoon pure vanilla extract until smooth. Stir in 1½ cups sifted confectioners' sugar, 2 tablespoons at a time, until creamy. Drizzle the finished pancakes with the frosting and sprinkle with chopped toasted walnuts.

SAUSAGE & WHITE CHEDDAR: Reduce the sugar to 2 teaspoons and add ½ teaspoon freshly ground black pepper to the dry ingredients. Fold 1 cup crumbled cooked breakfast sausage and ½ cup shredded white Cheddar cheese into the batter, just until incorporated.

BACON & CHIVE: Reduce the sugar to 1 teaspoon. Fold 1 cup crumbled cooked bacon (about 8 slices) and 2 thinly sliced green onions (white and green parts), into the batter, just until incorporated.

CHAI–WHOLE WHEAT: Stir 1 tablespoon chai tea mix into the buttermilk and let steep for 1 hour. Strain the buttermilk, discarding the tea, and use the chai-infused buttermilk in place of the regular buttermilk. Replace ⅔ cup of the all-purpose flour with ⅔ cup of the whole wheat flour. Whisk 1 teaspoon ground cardamom and ½ teaspoon ground cinnamon into the flour mixture.

CHOCOLATE CHIP & ORANGE: Fold ⅔ cup bittersweet chocolate chips and the grated zest and juice of 1 orange into the batter just until incorporated.

COCOA & CRANBERRY: Increase the sugar to 2½ tablespoons and whisk ⅓ cup natural unsweetened cocoa powder into the dry ingredients. Fold 1 cup dried cranberries into the batter, just until incorporated.

BLUEBERRY, LEMON & POPPY SEED: Stir the grated zest and juice of 1 lemon into the batter, then fold in 1 cup fresh blueberries and 1 tablespoon poppy seeds just until incorporated.

CLASSIC

RASPBERRY & RICOTTA

CARROT CAKE

SAUSAGE & WHITE CHEDDAR

BACON & CHIVE

CHAI–WHOLE WHEAT

CHOCOLATE CHIP & ORANGE

COCOA & CRANBERRY

BLUEBERRY, LEMON, &
POPPY SEED

DUTCH BABY

½ cup all-purpose flour

2 tablespoons superfine sugar

¼ teaspoon ground cinnamon

¼ teaspoon salt

Few gratings of nutmeg

2 eggs, lightly beaten

½ cup plus 2 tablespoons whole milk

4 tablespoons unsalted butter, melted

½ teaspoon pure vanilla extract

Confectioners' sugar, for dusting

I was out with friends at a local diner during junior high school when a waitress walked by carrying a small skillet holding a sweet-smelling, giant golden brown bubble dusted with loads of confectioners' sugar. We all looked at one another and said in unison, "Let's get that." I had no idea what "that" was, and I didn't care. About twenty minutes later, our own giant golden brown bubble was placed before us on the table. Five minutes later it was gone, and all we had to show for it were big smiles and a giant food coma. Now, I save Dutch babies for special days—days when I want to indulge, since I can devour a whole one myself! - Jenny

Place a 12-inch cast-iron or other ovenproof skillet in the oven and preheat the oven to 450°F.

Whisk together the flour, sugar, cinnamon, salt, and nutmeg in a bowl, mixing well. Add the eggs, milk, 1½ tablespoons of the butter, and the vanilla and whisk until smooth.

Using oven mitts, carefully remove the skillet from the oven and lower the oven temperature to 425°F. Add the remaining 2½ tablespoons of butter to the skillet, swirl to coat the bottom, and then pour the batter into the skillet. Quickly but carefully return the skillet to the oven and bake for 10 to 12 minutes, until puffed and golden brown.

Carefully remove the skillet from the oven, generously dust the top of the "bubble" with confectioners' sugar, and serve immediately.

SNACKS

CORN AND GREEN ONION FRITTERS WITH A BACON-HONEY DRIZZLE

BACON-HONEY DRIZZLE

½ cup honey

¼ cup finely crumbled cooked bacon

FRITTERS

Kernels from 3 ears corn (about 2 cups)

2 teaspoons extra-virgin olive oil

1½ cups water

2 tablespoons unsalted butter, at room temperature

1¼ teaspoons salt

1½ cups all-purpose flour

3 eggs

2 green onions, white and green parts, thinly sliced

½ teaspoon freshly ground black pepper

Canola oil, for deep-frying

While celebrating my sister's bachelorette weekend in the Bahamas, I feasted on copious amounts of conch fritters: chunks of the fresh mollusk dipped in batter, fried, and served with hot sauce and wedges of lime. The contrast of the light, crispy exterior and the rich, creamy interior was my idea of perfection. Back home in the States, we swapped out the hard-to-find conch for the corn and green onions you see here. But these fritters would be equally good made with chopped octopus or shrimp. - Jenny

To make the drizzle, stir together the honey and crumbled bacon in a bowl. Set aside.

To make the fritters, preheat the oven to 375°F. Line a baking sheet with parchment paper.

Put the corn kernels in a bowl, drizzle with the olive oil, and toss until the kernels are well coated. Spread the kernels in a single layer on the prepared baking sheet and roast, stirring once about halfway through the cooking time, for 15 to 20 minutes, until they begin to blister. Set aside.

Combine the water, butter, and salt in a saucepan and bring to a boil over medium-high heat. Add the flour and quickly stir with a wooden spoon until a dough forms. Continue to stir over medium heat for 3 minutes, until the dough begins to steam, becomes sticky, and pulls away from the sides of the pot.

Transfer the dough to a bowl and immediately beat with the wooden spoon for 2 minutes to allow the steam to escape. Add the eggs, one at a time, continuing to beat the mixture until the eggs are fully incorporated and scraping down the sides of the bowl after each addition. Fold in the green onions, pepper, and roasted corn.

To fry the fritters, pour canola oil into a deep pot to a depth of 2 inches and heat to 350°F. Line a large plate with paper towels and place near the stove.

Using a small ice cream scoop or 2 spoons, and working in batches of 4 or 6 fritters, carefully drop 2-tablespoon-sized balls of the corn mixture into the hot oil. Fry the balls, turning them once after 2 minutes, for 4 to 5 minutes, until golden brown. Using a slotted spoon, transfer the fritters to the paper-lined plate to drain, then sprinkle lightly with salt and pepper.

Transfer the fritters to a serving platter and top with the bacon-honey drizzle. Serve hot.

TIP: Between scoops of the fritter batter, dip your scoop or spoons into cold water to help prevent sticking and to ease the transfer of the balls to the hot oil.

PARMESAN POPCORN PUFFS

PÂTÉ À CHOUX

1½ cups water

1 tablespoon unsalted butter

1 teaspoon salt

1½ cups all-purpose flour

3 eggs

½ cup grated Parmesan cheese

½ teaspoon freshly ground black pepper

POPCORN PUREE

2 heaping cups unsalted popped popcorn

1 tablespoon grated Parmesan cheese

¼ teaspoon salt

½ cup unsalted butter, melted and cooled

Out for a night in downtown Chicago, a friend suggested an indulgent Champagne and cheese tasting, during which we ordered these puffs. When the puffs arrived, I mistook them for gougères (airy balls of choux pastry flavored with cheese), so I was taken by surprise when the first bite punched me in the face with an explosion of buttery popcorn flavor. To this day, I'm not sure how the kitchen created that irresistible bite infused with the essence of popcorn, but I think our version comes pretty close. - Jenny

Preheat the oven to 375°F. Line a baking sheet with parchment paper.

To make the pâte à choux, combine the water, butter, and salt in a saucepan and bring to a boil over medium-high heat. Add the flour and quickly stir with a wooden spoon until a dough forms. Continue to stir over medium heat for 3 minutes, until the dough becomes pale, sticky, and pulls away from the sides of the pot.

Transfer the dough to a bowl and immediately beat with the wooden spoon for about 2 minutes to allow the steam to escape. Add the eggs, one at a time, continuing to beat the mixture until fully incorporated, scraping down the sides of the bowl after each addition. Fold in the Parmesan and pepper.

Scoop the mixture into a large piping bag fitted with a ¼-inch plain tip, or into a gallon-sized resealable plastic bag with a corner snipped off to create a ¼-inch opening. Pipe quarter-sized mounds onto the prepared baking sheet, spacing them about 1 inch apart. Sprinkle the tops with the pepper and crushed popcorn.

Bake for 25 to 30 minutes, until golden brown. Turn off the oven, crack the oven door, and leave the puffs in the oven while you make the popcorn puree.

To make the popcorn puree, combine the popcorn, Parmesan, and salt in a food processor and pulse five times. Add 2 tablespoons of the butter and process until a puree forms. With the motor running, drizzle in the remaining 6 tablespoons of butter through the feed tube and process until a thick, smooth, and creamy puree forms. Transfer the puree to a squeeze bottle.

To fill the puffs, poke the tip of the squeeze bottle into the side of each puff and squeeze the bottle until the puff swells slightly. You will use about 1 teaspoon of puree for each puff. For the crispiest puffs, serve immediately.

TIP: The unfilled puffs can be baked up to 3 days in advance and stored in an airtight container, in a cool, dry place, away from direct sunlight. To serve, refresh them in a preheated 375°F oven for 5 to 7 minutes, let cool while making the filling, and then fill immediately before serving.

TEA EGGS

4½ cups water

12 eggs

½ cup soy sauce

3 tablespoons Oolong
tea leaves

3 star anise pods

2 cinnamon sticks

1 strip orange zest,
3 inches wide and
1 inch long

2 teaspoons
superfine sugar

We are enamored with the simplicity of this recipe, which yields complex flavor and great visual appeal. The mixture of tea, soy sauce, and aromatics seeps past the cracked shells to showcase the natural beauty of the eggs and to infuse them with the bath's delicate flavor. These eggs are tasty both warm and cold and make a fun and unique snack-on-the-go.

Bring the water to a boil in a stockpot. Using a ladle to prevent cracking, carefully lower the eggs into the water. Bring the water back to a slow boil and cook the eggs for 5 minutes.

Remove the pot from the heat. Using a slotted spoon, remove the eggs from the water and reserve the water in the pot. Allow eggs to cool just enough to be handled. Using the back of a spoon, gently tap each egg all over to crack the shell.

Add the soy sauce, tea, star anise, cinnamon, orange zest, and sugar to the reserved water and stir well. Return the eggs to the pot, place the pot over medium heat, bring to a slow boil, and cook the eggs for 10 minutes.

Remove the pot from the heat, cover, and let the eggs steep for at least 6 hours or for up to 10 hours. The longer the eggs steep, the fuller the flavor.

Remove the eggs from the liquid. The eggs can be served warm or cold. Always peel them just before serving. To serve the eggs warm, place a few of them (with their shells intact) in a heatproof bowl, pour in boiling water to cover, and cover the bowl. Let the eggs stand for about 10 minutes, then remove them from the water, peel, and serve.

Store leftover eggs in their shells in an airtight container in the refrigerator for up to 5 days.

MATCHA KIMI BALLS

⅔ cup potato starch

½ cup plus 1 tablespoon all-purpose flour

⅓ cup plus 2 tablespoons superfine sugar

Pinch of salt

¼ cup whole milk

2 teaspoons matcha (green tea powder)

3 tablespoons honey

1 egg yolk, at room temperature

Kimi balls, which originated in Japan and are also known as hachimitsu boro, hachimitsu balls, and honey biscuit balls, are like dense miniature biscuits, perfect for mindless snacking. Matcha, or green tea powder, adds a uniquely delicious and refreshing flavor. You can purchase matcha at most specialty tea stores and online. Some places offer a version specifically for baking, which is slightly lower in quality than the type used for making tea. Always store matcha in an airtight container in the refrigerator to keep it as fresh as possible.

Whisk together the potato starch, flour, sugar, and salt in a bowl, mixing well. Set aside.

Combine the milk, matcha, and honey in a small saucepan, bring to a simmer over medium-low heat, and simmer gently for 5 minutes. Remove from the heat, transfer to a bowl, and let cool completely.

Whisk the egg yolk into the cooled matcha mixture until fully incorporated. Add the potato starch mixture and stir until a smooth dough forms.

Preheat the oven to 350°F. Line a baking sheet with parchment paper.

To shape the balls, pinch off a ½-teaspoon-sized piece of the dough, roll between your palms into a smooth ball, and place on the prepared baking sheet, spacing the balls ½ inch apart.

Bake for 9 to 12 minutes, until puffed and barely browned. Let cool completely on the baking sheet before serving. Store the balls in an airtight container in a cool and dry place for up to 1 week.

GOCHU JEON

FILLING

8 ounces ground
lean beef

4 ounces firm tofu,
pressed and crumbled

2 cloves garlic, minced

1 green onion, white
and green parts, thinly
sliced

1½ teaspoons peeled
and minced fresh ginger

2 tablespoons soy sauce

1½ teaspoons toasted
sesame oil

½ teaspoon salt

¼ teaspoon freshly
ground black pepper

Pinch of superfine sugar

CHILES

8 Korean chiles

⅔ cup sweet rice flour

2 eggs

3 tablespoons
canola oil

Salt and freshly ground
black pepper

1 teaspoon black sesame
seeds, for garnish

This classic Korean snack of stuffed chiles is easy to make and packed with flavor. The stuffed peppers are great hot or at room temperature and will keep for up to a few days in the refrigerator. Although they are traditionally enjoyed as an appetizer or snack, we make a meal of them, accompanied with rice and kimchi.

Look for the chiles in Korean stores and other Asian markets. They are green and can vary in size from about 2 to 6 inches long, 1 to 2 inches in diameter, and in tastes from mild to medium hot. If you cannot find them, Anaheim chiles or pardon peppers can be substituted. You can also find sweet rice flour in Asian markets or in the Asian-foods aisle of well-stocked supermarkets. To press the tofu, wrap a small block in a few layers of cheesecloth and wring well until almost all of the excess water has been released.

To make the filling, combine the beef, tofu, garlic, green onion, ginger, soy sauce, sesame oil, salt, pepper, and sugar in a large bowl and mix well.

Cut off the stem and blossom end from each chile, then halve them lengthwise and remove and discard the seeds. Put the flour in a shallow bowl and toss the chiles in the flour, coating them evenly and shaking off the excess. Stuff the chile halves with the filling, dividing it evenly.

Crack the eggs into a shallow bowl and whisk until well blended. Heat the canola oil in a large skillet over medium-high heat. Dip half of the stuffed chiles into the beaten eggs, allowing the excess egg to drip off, and arrange them, beef side down, in the skillet. Cook for 3 to 4 minutes and then flip the chiles beef side up and continue to cook for 3 to 4 minutes longer, until the beef is cooked through. Transfer the chiles, beef side up, to a plate. Repeat with the remaining stuffed chiles and add them to the plate.

Season the chiles lightly with salt and pepper and sprinkle with the sesame seeds. Serve warm.

HOMEMADE CRACKERS

2 cups almond meal

⅔ cup sesame seeds

1½ tablespoons flaxseed meal

1 teaspoon minced fresh thyme

1 teaspoon salt, plus more for sprinkling

1 medium egg

1 medium egg yolk

1½ tablespoons coconut oil

My go-to snack in my elementary school years was Lunchables, a prepackaged meal stocked in supermarket cold cases and made up of crackers, cheese, and usually some type of processed meat. Although cheese and crackers remain a favorite snack, I'm not crazy about the idea of eating foods pumped up with artificial ingredients. My solution is these homemade crackers, which are not only more nutritious but are also easy to make and taste fantastic. Plus, they're gluten free! I enjoy them with cured meats and cheeses, enhanced with grainy mustard and briny gherkins, for my very own homemade grown-up Lunchables. - Jenny

Preheat the oven to 350°F.

Whisk together the almond meal, sesame seeds, flaxseed meal, thyme, and salt in a bowl, mixing well. In a small bowl, whisk together the egg, egg yolk, and coconut oil. Add the egg mixture to the almond meal mixture and stir until a slightly sticky dough forms.

Cut a sheet of parchment paper to fit a large baking sheet and lay the parchment on a work surface. Transfer the dough to the center of the parchment and cover the dough with a second piece of parchment of the same size. Roll out the dough into a rectangle 13 by 18 inches and about ⅛ inch thick. Remove and discard the top sheet of parchment and cut the dough into 1½-inch squares.

Transfer the bottom sheet of parchment with the squares to a baking sheet and lightly sprinkle the squares with salt. Bake for 9 to 12 minutes, until the crackers are light golden brown. Transfer the crackers on the parchment to a wire rack and let cool completely before breaking apart and serving.

The crackers will keep in an airtight container at room temperature for up to 2 weeks.

DEVILED EGGS

12 hard-boiled eggs
(page 11)

6 tablespoons
mayonnaise (page 15)

2½ teaspoons
Dijon mustard

1 teaspoon white
wine vinegar

¼ teaspoon salt

Pinch of
granulated sugar

Smoked paprika,
for garnish

Deviled eggs were a staple at special occasions of my youth. My mom made them simply and always the same way. I didn't realize until later that deviled eggs can be quite nuanced when made with a little extra thought. Although I still love mom's classic version, the variations that follow are also delicious. - Teri

Peel the eggs and halve them lengthwise. Scoop the egg yolks into a bowl and arrange the whites, hollow side up, on a platter. Add the mayonnaise, mustard, vinegar, salt, and sugar to the yolks and mash together with the back of a fork until no lumps remain. Using a spoon, scoop the yolk mixture into the whites, mounding it attractively. Alter-natively, spoon the yolk mixture into a piping bag fitted with whatever tip you prefer and pipe the filling into the egg whites. Sprinkle the tops with paprika and serve.

VARIATIONS:

PESTO: Mix 3 tablespoons pesto sauce into the yolk mixture.

DILL & PICKLE: Mix 2 tablespoons minced pickle (use whatever kind you like) and 1½ teaspoons minced fresh dill into the yolk mixture.

GINGER & SESAME: Mix 2 tablespoons minced pickled ginger; 1 teaspoon sesame seeds, toasted; and ¾ teaspoon toasted sesame oil into the yolk mixture by hand for a filling with some texture, or add the pickled ginger, sesame seeds, and sesame oil to the yolk mixture and process in a food processor until smooth.

THREE HERB: Use only 1 tablespoon mayonnaise. Mix ¼ cup crumbled fresh goat cheese and ½ teaspoon each minced fresh marjoram, thinly sliced fresh chives, and minced fresh thyme into the yolk mixture.

SAUTÉED SHALLOT & PANCETTA: Melt 2 tablespoons unsalted butter in a small skillet over medium heat. Heat, swirling the pan occasionally, for about 2 minutes, until the butter begins to brown and smells nutty. Add 3 tablespoons minced shallots and sauté for 3 minutes, until barely translucent. Mix the shallots and 2 tablespoons crumbled cooked pancetta into the yolk mixture by hand for a filling with some texture, or add the shallots and pancetta to the yolk mixture and process in a food processor until smooth.

BUFFALO: Mix 2½ tablespoons Frank's Red Hot Sauce and 1½ tablespoons crumbled blue cheese into the yolk mixture by hand for a filling with some texture, or add the hot sauce and blue cheese to the yolk mixture and process in a food processor until smooth.

SUN-DRIED TOMATO: Mix 3 tablespoons minced dry-packed sun-dried tomato and 2 teaspoons crumbled feta cheese into the yolk mixture.

SRIRACHA & CRACKED PEPPER: Mix 2½ tablespoons Sriracha sauce, 1½ teaspoons minced shallot, and ½ teaspoon cracked black pepper into the yolk mixture.

PESTO

CLASSIC

DILL & PICKLE

GINGER & SESAME

THREE HERB

SAUTÉED SHALLOT
& PANCETTA

BUFFALO

SUN-DRIED
TOMATO

SRIRACHA &
CRACKED PEPPER

BEEF TARTARE

6 ounces filet
mignon, minced

1½ teaspoons black
sesame seeds

2 teaspoons freshly
squeezed lemon juice

1 teaspoon salt

1 teaspoon toasted
sesame oil, plus
1 tablespoon, for
garnish

3 quail egg yolks, or
1 chicken egg yolk

Grated zest of 2 lemons

1 teaspoon freshly
ground black pepper

Microgreens,
for garnish

Toasted pine nuts,
for garnish

Sourdough toast points

I don't make any type of tartare often, and when I do, I really want to get it right. Of the many versions of this popular dish made throughout the world, my favorite is this take on a Korean-style tartare, rich with egg yolks and the flavor of nutty sesame oil. I use quail egg yolks, both for presentation and for flavor control, but it is fine to replace them with a chicken egg yolk. Because the egg yolks are raw, make sure the eggs you use are at the peak of freshness and are from a trustworthy purveyor. Seek out the highest-quality filet mignon, as well. - Jenny

Combine the filet mignon, sesame seeds, lemon juice, salt, and sesame oil in a bowl and stir until well mixed.

If using the quail egg yolks, spread the beef mixture across a serving plate and top with the yolks, spacing them evenly apart. If using a single chicken egg yolk, form the tartare into a short, wide cylinder, gently press a shallow indentation into the center of the top, and place the egg in the indentation.

In a small bowl, stir together the lemon zest and pepper, then sprinkle over the tartare. Top with the microgreens and pine nuts and a drizzle of sesame oil, and serve family style with the toast points.

TIP: For added texture and flavor, stir ½ cup diced, peeled Asian pear to the beef mixture.

SWEET POTATO–EGG SHOAP

RAITA

¾ cup coarsely grated, peeled cucumber

½ cup plain full-fat Greek yogurt

grated zest and juice of ½ lemon

1 teaspoon honey

½ teaspoon salt

¼ teaspoon ground cumin

Pinch of smoked paprika

CROQUETTES

1½ cups mashed cooked sweet potatoes

2 hard-boiled eggs (page 11), peeled and cut into ½-inch chunks

½ yellow onion, diced

2 cloves garlic, minced

1½ teaspoons minced fresh thyme

1 teaspoon ground cumin

½ teaspoon ground coriander

¼ teaspoon ground turmeric

Salt and freshly ground black pepper

2 egg whites

1 cup dried bread crumbs

canola oil, for deep-frying

A shoap is a type of potato-and-egg croquette popular in the northeastern Indian state of Assam. To fancy up the croquettes, we swap out the usual white potatoes in favor of mashed sweet potatoes, and we serve them with a creamy-cool raita dipping sauce. They are best eaten piping hot—right out of the oil.

To make the raita, stir together the cucumber, yogurt, lemon zest and juice, honey, salt, cumin, and paprika in a small bowl. Cover and refrigerate for at least 2 hours, then let stand at room temperature for 10 minutes before serving.

To make the croquettes, combine the sweet potatoes, eggs, onion, garlic, thyme, cumin, coriander, and turmeric in a large bowl and mix well. Season with salt and pepper.

Put the egg whites in a small, shallow bowl and beat lightly. Put the bread crumbs in a second small, shallow bowl. Scoop ¼ cup of the potato-egg mixture into your hands and form into a small patty about 2 ½ inches in diameter and ½ inch thick. Gently dip the patty into the egg whites, allowing the excess to drip off, and then into the bread crumbs, coating evenly and shaking off any excess crumbs. Set the patty aside on a large plate. Repeat with the remaining mixture to form a total of 12 patties.

Pour the oil into a deep pot to a depth of 2 inches and heat to 350°F. Line a large plate with paper towels and place near the stove.

Gently lower 3 or 4 patties into the oil and fry, turning the patties once, for 2 to 3 minutes on each side, until golden all over. Using a slotted spoon, transfer to the paper-lined plate to drain and season with salt and pepper. Repeat with the remaining patties.

Arrange the croquettes on a large plate and serve warm with bowls of the raita for dipping.

TIP: Dip your hands into a bowl of cool water before forming each patty to help prevent sticking.

HERB AND CHEESE MACARONS

FILLING

½ cup mascarpone cheese, at room temperature

¼ cup shredded Gruyère cheese

2 tablespoons whole milk

1½ teaspoons white wine vinegar

1½ teaspoons minced fresh thyme

1 teaspoon thinly sliced fresh chives

¼ teaspoon freshly ground black pepper

MACARONS

1 cup almond meal

1 cup sifted confectioners' sugar

2 tablespoons beetroot powder

½ teaspoon salt

4 egg whites, at room temperature

⅓ cup plus 2 tablespoons superfine sugar

Fresh thyme leaves, for garnish

These are the savory answer to the explosively popular sweet French *macarons*. We love the balance between the delicate melt-in-your mouth exterior and the creamy herb filling that awakens the taste buds. Get creative and substitute the herbs you like for what we have used here.

To make the filling, combine the mascarpone, Gruyère, milk, vinegar, thyme, chives, and pepper in a food processor and process until completely smooth. Scoop into a bowl, cover, and set aside.

To make the macarons, preheat the oven to 300°F. Line a baking sheet with parchment paper.

Sift together the almond meal, confectioners' sugar, beetroot powder, and salt into a bowl. Discard any clumps remaining in the sieve. In a separate large bowl, combine the egg whites and superfine sugar and beat with a stand mixer or handheld mixer on medium-high speed, or by hand with a whisk, until medium-stiff peaks form. Sift the almond meal mixture over the egg whites, then, using a rubber spatula, gently fold the mixtures together until no white streaks remain. It's okay if the egg whites lose a bit of air.

Scoop the mixture into a large piping bag fitted with a ½-inch plain tip, or into a gallon-sized resealable plastic bag with one corner snipped to create a ½-inch opening. Pipe 40 quarter-sized mounds onto the prepared baking sheet, spacing them about 1 inch apart. Tap the baking sheet on a flat surface to release excess air bubbles from the mounds. Top each mound with a few fresh thyme leaves.

Bake for 8 minutes, then rotate the baking sheet back to front and continue to bake for 8 to 10 minutes longer, until you see the top of each mound smooth out and the bottom grow "feet." Remove from the oven and let cool completely on the baking sheet, then carefully remove the macaroons from the parchment.

Do not fill the macarons until you are ready to serve them. They will keep in an airtight container at room temperature for up to 3 days, and the filling can be stored in an airtight container in the refrigerator for up to a week. Then, just before serving, spread the bottom of half of the macarons with the filling, dividing it evenly. Top with the second half of each macaron, bottom side down. Arrange the filled macarons on a platter and serve.

AFTERNOON

CHAWANMUSHI

2 cups dashi or vegetable stock

1½ teaspoons soy sauce

1 teaspoon mirin (sweet rice wine)

½ teaspoon bakers' sugar

4 eggs

2 ounces shiitake mushrooms, stems discarded and caps thinly sliced

1 green onion, white and green parts, cut lengthwise into thirds and then thinly sliced crosswise, for garnish

The eggs take on a soft, creamy texture yet maintain their body in this savory steamed egg custard dish from Japan. Chinese and Korean cooks make their own versions of this addictive comfort food, and you can too, by adding other vegetables, such as carrots or snow peas, or even small shrimp or chunks of chicken. We prefer to keep our version simple so the silky egg custard is the star. You will need four small lidded, heatproof bowls for steaming the custard, or you can make one large custard in a bowl, using a flat plate as the lid.

Combine the dashi, soy sauce, mirin, and sugar in a saucepan and bring to a simmer over medium heat. Let simmer for 5 minutes, then remove from the heat, and let cool.

Whisk the eggs in a bowl until well blended. While whisking constantly, add the cooled stock to the eggs in a slow, steady stream, continuing to whisk until fully incorporated and perfectly smooth.

Divide the mushrooms evenly among 4 small lidded, heatproof bowls. Fill each bowl three-fourths full with the broth-egg mixture. Cover the bowls with their lids.

Bring water to a simmer in a steamer pan over medium-low heat. Place the steamer rack over, not touching, the water, and place the bowls on the rack, spacing them at least ½ inch apart. Cover the steamer and cook for 12 to 15 minutes, until the custards are gently set.

Remove the bowls from the steamer and let them stand, covered, for 5 minutes. Meanwhile, put the green onion slices into a small bowl of ice water to curl.

Drain the green onion slices and then grab them, a few at a time, and shake them well to remove any excess water. Garnish the custards with the green onion slices and serve immediately.

HOT AND SOUR SOUP

4 cups chicken stock

½ cup plus 1 tablespoon soy sauce

1 tablespoon peeled and grated fresh ginger

2 cloves garlic, minced

1 teaspoon Asian-style chile paste (such as sambal oelek)

½ teaspoon ground white pepper

½ cup loosely packed brown beech mushrooms

1 carrot, peeled and cut into julienne

1 (4 ounce) can (about ¾ cup) sliced bamboo shoots, drained and cut into julienne

¼ cup cornstarch

3 tablespoons water

¼ cup rice vinegar

¼ teaspoon superfine sugar

2 eggs, lightly beaten

Meat from one poached or roasted chicken breast, finely shredded (optional)

2 green onions, white and green parts, thinly sliced, for garnish

Los Angeles's Koreatown, where I live, is a hub of amazing food, much of it coming from hole-in-the wall Korean or Korean-Chinese restaurants. When I feel a cold coming on, or I just feel downhearted, my go-to remedy is hot and sour soup, which I often pick up for six dollars a quart at the little restaurant down the street. It's one of the most comforting, soothing, and tasty soups I know and is the perfect substitute for the more common tonic, chicken soup. - Teri

Combine the stock, soy sauce, ginger, garlic, chile paste, and white pepper in a medium pot and bring to a boil over medium-high heat. Stir in the mushrooms, carrot, and bamboo shoots, lower the heat to medium-low, and simmer for 10 minutes.

Whisk together the cornstarch and water in a small bowl to form a slurry. Stir the slurry into the soup and continue to simmer, stirring occasionally, for about 5 minutes, until the soup thickens slightly. Stir in the vinegar and sugar, then add the eggs in a slow, steady stream while stirring the soup constantly. The eggs should form a mixture of fine shreds and thin ribbons.

Remove from the heat, add the chicken, and stir gently to heat through. Taste and adjust the seasoning, ladle into warmed bowls, and garnish with the green onions. Serve immediately.

AVGOLEMONO SOUP

4 cups chicken stock

¼ cup orzo pasta

1 egg

2 egg yolks

Grated zest and juice of 1 lemon, plus more grated zest, for garnish

Salt and freshly ground black pepper

My first taste of avgolemono soup was at a restaurant in Chicago's Greektown, when I was feeling under the weather and craved a bowl of hot broth. From the menu description, I expected something like a lemon-scented egg drop soup. But what came to the table was a thick, creamy soup flecked with orzo and fragrant with lemon. I was completely surprised and immediately seduced. For a heartier meal, stir in shredded cooked chicken breast just before serving. - Jenny

Pour the stock into a saucepan and bring to a boil over medium-high heat. Stir in the orzo and boil for 6 to 8 minutes, until al dente.

While the orzo cooks, whisk together the egg, egg yolks, and lemon zest and juice in a bowl until foamy and pale yellow. When the orzo is ready, pour ½ cup of the hot stock into the egg mixture in a slow, steady stream while whisking constantly. Lower the heat to medium-low and slowly pour the egg-soup mixture back into the saucepan while whisking constantly.

Simmer the soup gently, stirring frequently, for 8 to 10 minutes, until thick enough to coat the back of a wooden spoon. Season with salt and pepper, then ladle into warmed bowls, garnish with lemon zest, and serve immediately.

UPDATED SALADE LYONNAISE

ANCHOVY VINAIGRETTE

2 oil-packed anchovy fillets, minced

1 clove garlic, minced

3 tablespoons minced shallot

2 tablespoons whole-grain mustard

2 teaspoons mild honey

⅓ to ½ cup extra-virgin olive oil

Salt and freshly ground black pepper

SALAD

½ teaspoon extra-virgin olive oil

8 ounces pancetta, chopped

4 eggs

1 head chicory or frisée, core removed and roughly chopped

Salt and freshly ground black pepper

Grated lemon zest, for garnish

In our update of this classic French salad, bitter chicory, salty pancetta, and creamy poached eggs are cloaked in a creamy-briny anchovy vinaigrette for an ideal balance of flavor and texture.

To make the vinaigrette, stir together the anchovies, garlic, shallot, mustard, and honey in a small bowl. While whisking constantly, drizzle in ⅓ cup of the oil in a slow, steady stream until it is fully incorporated and the vinaigrette is emulsified. If the vinaigrette is too thick, whisk in the remaining oil. Season with salt and pepper and set aside.

Heat the oil in a skillet over medium heat. Add the pancetta and cook, stirring occasionally, for 5 to 7 minutes, until the fat has rendered and the pancetta is crisp. Using a slotted spoon, transfer the pancetta to paper towels to drain.

Poach the eggs as directed on page 12.

To finish the salad, put the chicory in a large bowl, drizzle with the vinaigrette, and toss to coat evenly. Divide the greens among 4 plates and top each bed of greens with one-fourth of the pancetta and a poached egg. Season each serving lightly with salt and pepper and top with a few gratings of lemon zest.

CHARRED CAESAR SALAD

CROUTONS

1 cup cubed sourdough bread, in ½-inch cubes

3 tablespoons extra-virgin olive oil

1 teaspoon minced fresh thyme

½ teaspoon salt

¼ teaspoon freshly ground black pepper

DRESSING

5 oil-packed anchovy fillets, mashed into a paste

2 cloves garlic, minced

½ teaspoon Dijon mustard

2 egg yolks

Juice of ½ lemon

3 tablespoons extra-virgin olive oil

½ cup canola oil

1 tablespoon grated Parmesan cheese

Salt and freshly ground black pepper

SALAD

2 to 3 romaine hearts, trimmed and halved lengthwise

2 tablespoons extra-virgin olive oil

Salt and freshly ground black pepper

2 ounces Parmesan cheese, shaved

The Caesar is my favorite salad, and when I make it, I take my dressing seriously. Easy to make, it is creamier and more flavorful than any dressing you will find at the store, and it carries a deliciously briny kick from anchovies brightened by fresh lemon juice. Once you try our version, you will never go back to the bottle! - Teri

To make the croutons, put the bread cubes in a bowl, drizzle with the oil, and add the thyme, salt, and pepper. Toss to coat the bread cubes evenly.

Place a large skillet over medium-low heat and spread the bread cubes in a single layer in the pan. Toast, stirring frequently, for 6 to 7 minutes, until light golden brown all over. Transfer the croutons to a plate and let cool.

To make the dressing, whisk together the anchovies, garlic, and mustard in a bowl. Add the egg yolks and continue to whisk until the mixture is light and slightly thickened; then whisk in the lemon juice. Add the olive oil, a few drops at a time, whisking to incorporate fully after each addition. Add the canola oil in a slow, steady stream while whisking constantly. Stir in the Parmesan and then taste and adjust the seasoning.

To char the lettuce, heat a stove-top grill pan over high heat or prepare a hot fire in a charcoal or gas grill. Brush the halved romaine hearts with olive oil, season them lightly with salt and pepper, and then place them, cut side down, on the grill pan or grill rack. Cook, turning them once, for about 2 minutes on each side, until the hearts just begin to char but remain crisp.

To finish the salad, transfer the romaine hearts to a platter and drizzle with the dressing. Serve topped with the croutons and Parmesan.

NO LEAFY GREENS SALAD

BALSAMIC VINAIGRETTE

2 tablespoons minced shallot

1 clove garlic, minced

2 teaspoons light brown sugar

1 teaspoon Dijon mustard

½ cup balsamic vinegar

⅔ cup extra-virgin olive oil

Salt and freshly ground black pepper to taste

SALAD

1 cup uncooked farro, rinsed and drained

4 cups chicken stock

Salt

8 baby zucchini, sliced in half lengthwise

10 French green beans, sliced in half lengthwise

2 radishes, trimmed and thinly sliced

4 soft boiled eggs, halved (see page 11)

Microgreens, crushed pistachios, and grated lemon zest, for garnish

When the quinoa explosion hit the United States about a decade ago, it seemed to overshadow a number of other, just as tasty and nutritious grains. Don't get me wrong, I love both the flavor and texture of cooked quinoa, but personally, I hold farro in higher regard. The pleasantly chewy texture is what really gets me excited about farro and I love pairing it with a variety of vegetables. While I was in culinary school, this salad was my go-to meal. I was usually able to cook a little extra farro at school and sneak it home, and since I was often at the local farmer's market, my refrigerator at home was usually packed with fresh, seasonal produce. The egg on top really turns this light grain salad into a complete meal that's completely satisfying. - Jenny

Place all the vinaigrette ingredients, except the olive oil, into a small mixing bowl and whisk together. While whisking, pour in the oil in a slow and steady stream. Continue to whisk until the mixture has emulsified. Taste, adjust the seasoning if needed, and set aside until ready to use.

Pour the farro and stock into a medium pot and bring to a boil. Once the stock has come to a boil, reduce heat to medium and simmer for 30 to 40 minutes or until most of the liquid has been absorbed and the grains have softened and split. Drain any remaining liquid and allow the farro to cool, about 1 hour.

Fill a small pot with water and bring to a boil. Once water has boiled, generously season with salt and drop in the zucchini and French green beans. Blanch vegetables for 2 to 3 minutes and then transfer them to an ice bath to ensure the vegetables retain some texture. Once cooled, drain the vegetables and place into a large mixing bowl with the cooked farro and sliced radishes. Drizzle half of the vinaigrette over the mixture and toss together (you can reserve the remaining vinaigrette for another use). Top the salad with microgreens, crushed pistachios, and grated lemon zest, and serve.

TIP: To cool farro quickly, spread onto a sheet pan, in a thin layer, and place in the refrigerator for about 15 minutes.

CAPER & DILL

OLIVE & WHOLE-GRAIN MUSTARD

BACON, AVOCADO & RED ONION

FOUR HERB

GREEN ONION & SESAME

CURRY

JALAPEÑO & CILANTRO

EGG WHITE

CLASSIC

EGG SALAD SANDWICHES

8 hard-boiled eggs
(page 11)

2 tablespoons diced
dill pickle

3 tablespoons
mayonnaise (page 15)

2 teaspoons Dijon
mustard

1½ teaspoons thinly
sliced fresh chives

½ teaspoon cider
vinegar

¼ teaspoon salt

¼ teaspoon freshly
ground black pepper

8 slices country white
bread, lightly toasted

What was once one of my mom's standard lunches has morphed into an adult favorite. When I was a child and my body ached from after-school sports, my mom would fry an egg and then sandwich it between two slices of white bread slathered with mayo. It was my comfort food. My grown-up versions are these egg salad variations, all of which are made with ingredients that are usually on hand. - Teri

Peel and chop the eggs and place in a bowl. Add the pickle, mayonnaise, mustard, chives, vinegar, salt, and pepper and mix well.

Divide the egg salad evenly among 4 toast slices and top with the remaining 4 toast slices. Press gently and then cut each sandwich in half.

VARIATIONS:

CAPER & DILL: Stir 1 tablespoon diced capers and 1½ teaspoons minced fresh dill into the egg mixture.

OLIVE & WHOLE-GRAIN MUSTARD: Replace the Dijon mustard with 1½ tablespoons whole-grain mustard and stir 1½ tablespoons chopped Castelvetrano olives and 1 tablespoon chopped black olives into the egg mixture.

BACON, AVOCADO & RED ONION: Replace the hard-boiled eggs with soft-boiled eggs. Omit the chives and stir 2½ tablespoons crumbled cooked bacon; ¼ avocado, peeled and diced; and 1½ tablespoons minced red onion into the egg mixture.

FOUR HERB: Reduce the chives to 1 teaspoon. Stir 1 teaspoon each minced fresh thyme, oregano, and sage into the egg mixture.

GREEN ONION & SESAME: Replace the hard-boiled eggs with soft-boiled eggs. Omit the mustard and chives and stir 1 teaspoon toasted sesame oil; 1 teaspoon sesame seeds, toasted; and 1½ green onions, white and green parts, thinly sliced, into the egg mixture.

CURRY: Replace the hard-boiled eggs with soft-boiled eggs. Omit the mustard and chives and stir 2 teaspoons curry powder and ½ teaspoon ground cumin into the egg mixture.

JALAPEÑO & CILANTRO: Stir 2 tablespoons diced, seeded jalapeño chile and 1 tablespoon minced fresh cilantro into the egg mixture.

EGG WHITE: Omit all of the egg yolks, add 2 additional hard-boiled egg whites, and replace the black pepper with white pepper.

BEEF EMPANADAS

DOUGH

2¼ cups flour

1½ teaspoons salt

½ cup cold unsalted butter, cut into cubes

1 egg

⅓ cup ice water

1 tablespoon cider vinegar

FILLING

2 tablespoons extra-virgin olive oil

½ poblano chile, seeded and diced

⅓ cup fresh corn kernels

¼ yellow onion, diced

1 Roma tomato, seeded and diced

1 clove garlic, minced

8 ounces ground beef

1½ teaspoons tomato paste

1 tablespoon plus 1 teaspoon minced fresh oregano

Salt and freshly ground black pepper

3 hard-boiled eggs (page 11), peeled and chopped

20 Castelvetrano or other brine-cured green olives, pitted and chopped

1 egg, lightly beaten with 2 tablespoons water, for egg wash

Canola oil, for deep-frying

We are crazy for this Argentinean version of these folded pockets, made by incorporating hard-boiled eggs and olives into the filling. You can make the empanadas; freeze them, well wrapped, for up to 2 months; and then fry them (without defrosting) when you're hungry.

To make the dough, whisk together the flour and salt in a bowl. Scatter the butter over the flour mixture. Then, using two knives or a pastry blender, cut in the butter until the mixture is fine and grainy. Whisk together the egg, water, and vinegar in a small bowl. Pour the egg mixture into the flour mixture and stir them together with a wooden spoon until the dough comes together in a rough mass.

Lightly flour a work surface. Turn the dough out onto the floured surface and knead briefly until smooth, taking care not to handle it excessively so the pastry remains tender. Form the dough into a thick disk, wrap in plastic wrap, and refrigerate for at least 1 hour or up to 2 days.

To make the filling, heat the olive oil in a large skillet over medium-high heat. When the oil is hot, add the chile, corn, onion, tomato, and garlic and sauté for about 3 minutes, until fragrant. Add the beef and continue to sauté, breaking up the meat with a wooden spoon and stirring, for about 6 minutes longer, until the beef has browned. Stir in the tomato paste and oregano and season with salt and pepper. Lower the heat to medium-low and stir in the eggs and olives, mixing well. Remove from the heat and taste and adjust the seasoning. Let the filling cool for at least 30 minutes before filling the empanadas.

To fill the empanadas, lightly flour a work surface, unwrap the dough disk, and place it on the floured surface. Allow dough to sit for about 15 minutes before rolling it out to about ⅛ inch thick. Using a 5- to 6-inch round cutter, cut out as many rounds as possible. Set the rounds aside, gather dough scraps, and reroll until ⅛ inch thick. Cut remaining rounds from the dough.

Brush the entire edge of a dough round with the egg wash, then put ¼ to ⅓ cup of the filling into the center of the round. Fold the dough over the filling to make a half-moon and crimp the edges together tightly with a fork to seal securely. Repeat to fill the remaining dough rounds.

To fry the empanadas, pour the canola oil into a deep pot to a depth of 3 inches and heat to 350°F. Line a large plate with paper towels and place near the stove.

Gently lower 3 or 4 empanadas into the hot oil and fry for about 5 minutes, until golden brown. Using a slotted spoon, transfer to the towel-lined plate to drain. Repeat with the remaining empanadas. Serve hot.

GARLIC AND GREEN ONION NOODLE KUGEL

1 pound wide
egg noodles

5 eggs

1¼ cups sour cream

1¼ cups cottage cheese

⅔ cup shredded
mozzarella cheese

¼ cup grated Parmesan
cheese

3 cloves garlic, minced

3 green onions, white
and green parts, thinly
sliced

¼ teaspoon freshly
ground black pepper

Although noodle kugel is better known as a sweet, rich pudding studded with raisins, we think that it is at its best when it flaunts its savory side. Enriched with three kinds of cheese, this version makes a satisfying main dish or an accompaniment to pot roast, roasted duck, or braised chicken. This recipe makes enough to feed a large family, but it also freezes and reheats quite well for those in need of eating this in batches.

Preheat the oven to 375°F. Brush a 9-by 13-inch baking dish with 6 tablespoons unsalted butter, melted, cooled, and divided.

Fill a large pot three-fourths full with water and bring to a boil over high heat. Add 1 teaspoon of the salt and then stir in the noodles. Bring the water back to a boil and cook the noodles, stirring occasionally, for 6 to 8 minutes, until al dente. Drain well.

While the noodles are cooking, use a large bowl to whisk together the eggs, sour cream, cottage cheese, mozzarella, Parmesan, garlic, green onions, the remaining 1¾ teaspoon salt, the pepper, and the remaining 4 tablespoons butter until well mixed. Add the drained noodles and mix until all of the ingredients are evenly distributed.

Scrape the mixture into the prepared baking dish. Bake for 30 to 35 minutes, until the kugel is set and the top is golden brown. Let cool for 7 to 10 minutes before cutting and serving.

TIP: You can assemble the kugel in advance, cover it tightly with plastic wrap, and refrigerate it for up to 2 days or freeze it for up to 2 months. If refrigerated, let it stand at room temperature for 30 minutes and then remove the plastic wrap and bake as directed. If frozen, place kugel directly in the oven and bake for an additional 15 minutes.

NIGHT

CROQUE-MADAME

MORNAY SAUCE

1 tablespoon
unsalted butter

1 tablespoon
all-purpose flour

½ cup plus 2 tablespoons
whole milk

½ teaspoon dry mustard

½ teaspoon ground
ginger

⅓ cup shredded
Gruyère cheese

3 tablespoons grated
Parmesan cheese

Salt and freshly ground
black pepper

SANDWICHES

3 tablespoons whole-
grain mustard

4 slices French bread,
lightly toasted

6 ounces smoked ham,
thinly sliced

¼ cup shredded
Gruyère cheese

2 eggs

Salt and freshly ground
black pepper

For a few months in college, I worked at a French restaurant that had a croque-madame on the menu. The sandwich is one of those ultimate indulgences that leave you dreaming of the next time you get to eat one. At the end of every busy Sunday-morning shift, I would reward myself with a croque-madame. I dreaded that stressful shift, but the thought of my knife plunging through layers of egg, buttered toast, ham, Gruyère, and Mornay sauce got me through the day and even made the hustle all worthwhile. - Teri

To make the sauce, melt the butter in a small saucepan over medium heat. Stir in the flour and cook, stirring, for 2 to 3 minutes to cook off the raw flour taste. While whisking constantly, pour in the milk in a slow, steady stream. Continue to cook, whisking constantly, for 1 to 2 minutes, until the mixture thickens enough to coat the back of a wooden spoon. Whisk in the mustard, ginger, Gruyère, and Parmesan and continue to cook and stir for 3 to 4 minutes, until the cheeses melt and the sauce is smooth. Season with salt and pepper and set aside.

Preheat the broiler. Spread the mustard onto one side of each toast slice. Top 2 toast slices with the ham, dividing it evenly, and then sprinkle the Gruyère evenly over the ham, again dividing it evenly. Close the sandwiches with the remaining 2 toast slices.

Transfer the sandwiches to a baking sheet and top each sandwich with ½ cup of the Mornay sauce. Broil the sandwiches for 4 to 5 minutes, until the sauce is hot and bubbling.

Meanwhile, fry the eggs in butter as directed on page 12.

Place 1 egg on top of each sandwich. Season lightly with salt and pepper and serve immediately.

DOLSOT BIBIMBAP

SIGUMCHI NAMUL (SEASONED SPINACH)

1 tablespoon soy sauce

2 teaspoons toasted sesame oil

2 cloves garlic, minced

¼ teaspoon sesame seeds, toasted

1 pound spinach, tough stems removed, blanched, drained, and wrung dry

Salt and freshly ground black pepper

SUKJU NAMUL (BEAN SPROUTS)

1 teaspoon toasted sesame oil

1 clove garlic, minced

½ teaspoon salt

¼ teaspoon freshly ground black pepper

1 green onion, white and green parts, thinly sliced

¼ teaspoon sesame seeds, toasted

1 pound mung bean sprouts, blanched and pressed to remove excess liquid

ZUCCHINI AND CARROTS

2 small zucchini, trimmed and grated

Salt and freshly ground black pepper

2 tablespoons canola oil

Bibimbap (literally "mixed rice"), a loaded rice bowl finished with a fried egg, is my chicken soup. It's the ultimate comfort dish. In dolsot bibimbap, the rice is topped with mounds of various prepared vegetables and marinated beef, seasoned with spicy chile paste, and served in a scorching hot stone bowl (see tip) that crisps the edges of the rice. A fried egg brings all of the elements together in sizzling perfection. Don't be put off by the many subrecipes in this recipe, as they are all quick and easy to make. Gochujang is a spicy Korean chile paste that packs great flavor. Look for it in Korean markets or in the Asian-foods aisle of well-stocked supermarkets. You can make the gochujang paste up to 3 days in advance and refrigerate it in an airtight container. - Jenny

To make the spinach, whisk together the soy sauce, sesame oil, garlic, and sesame seeds in a bowl. Add the spinach and mix until thoroughly coated with the sauce. Season with salt and pepper. Set aside.

To make the bean sprouts, whisk together the sesame oil, garlic, salt, pepper, green onion, and sesame seeds in a bowl. Add the bean sprouts and mix until thoroughly coated with the sauce. Set aside.

To make the zucchini and carrots, put the zucchini in a bowl and season with salt and pepper. Heat 1 tablespoon of the canola oil and 1 teaspoon of the sesame oil in a skillet over medium-high heat. When the oil is hot, add the zucchini and sauté for 3 to 4 minutes, until softened but not soggy. Transfer to a plate and set aside. Season and then cook the carrots in the same way, using the remaining 1 tablespoon of canola oil and 1 teaspoon of sesame oil and cooking for 4 to 5 minutes, until softened. Transfer to a separate plate and set aside.

To make the bulgogi, put the beef and onion in a bowl. Combine the pureed Asian pear, soy sauce, mirin, sesame oil, honey, garlic, and pepper in a blender and puree until smooth. Pour the puree over the beef and onion and mix well, coating the meat and onion evenly. Cover and marinate at room temperature for 30 minutes.

Heat the oil in a skillet over medium-high heat. Add the marinated beef and sear, turning once, for 3 to 4 minutes on each side, until just cooked through. Transfer the meat to a cutting board and cut into long slices. Set aside.

To make the gochujang paste, whisk together the gochujang, sesame oil, vinegar, sugar, and garlic in a small bowl until thoroughly combined.

To assemble the bibimbap, divide the sesame oil evenly between 2 dolsot bowls

2 small carrots, peeled and grated

2 teaspoons toasted sesame oil

BULGOGI (GRILLED BEEF)

8 ounces boneless rib-eye steak, thinly sliced

¼ yellow onion, thinly sliced

½ Asian pear, peeled and pureed (about ½ cup puree)

3 tablespoons reduced-sodium soy sauce

1½ tablespoons mirin (sweet rice wine)

1 tablespoon toasted sesame oil

2 teaspoons honey

2 cloves garlic

½ teaspoon freshly ground black pepper

2 tablespoons canola oil

GOCHUJANG PASTE

3 tablespoons gochujang (Korean chile paste)

1 tablespoon toasted sesame oil

2 teaspoons rice vinegar

2 teaspoons superfine sugar

1 clove garlic, minced

TOPPING

1 tablespoon toasted sesame oil

1½ cups hot, steamed brown rice

2 eggs

1 green onion, white and green parts, thinly sliced

1 teaspoon sesame seeds, toasted

(see tip) and then divide the rice evenly between the bowls. Top the rice in each bowl with small mounds of the prepared spinach, bean sprouts, zucchini, carrots, and beef, arranging the mounds around the perimeter of each bowl and leaving a space in the center.

Place the bowls on the stove top over high heat and cook for 3 to 4 minutes, until the rice on the bottom begins to crisp (you will hear popping sounds) and the bowls are extremely hot. Crack an egg into the center of each bowl and continue to cook for about 3 minutes, until the white is opaque and the yolk is still runny.

Using oven mitts, carefully transfer the hot bowls to a heat-resistant surface. Serve garnished with the green onion and sesame seeds and with a warning that the bowls are scorching hot!

TIP: Dolsot bowls are heavy stoneware bowls used specifically for bibimbap. They are designed to be placed directly over a flame so that a crispy rice layer forms on the bottom of the bowl and anything directly touching the sides of the bowl heats up. You can find them at most local Korean markets or online, usually for twelve to twenty dollars each. A cast-iron or nonstick skillet can be substituted.

SHRIMP OKONOMIYAKI

1½ cups loosely packed, thinly sliced Savoy or napa cabbage

1 carrot, peeled and thinly sliced

2 green onions, white and green parts, thinly sliced

1¼ cups all-purpose flour

3 eggs, lightly beaten

¾ cup dashi or water

½ teaspoon salt

¼ teaspoon ground white pepper

12 medium-sized shrimp, peeled, deveined, and coarsely chopped

2 tablespoons canola oil

Okonomiyaki sauce, for garnish

Mayonnaise (page 15), for garnish

Furikake seasoning, for garnish

Dried bonito flakes, for garnish

On a visit to San Francisco for work, we enjoyed a memorable okonomiyaki. We were at the Saturday farmers' market at the Ferry Building, and a friend walked up holding a beautifully decorated omelet-pancake, a crazy concoction covered in squiggles of various sauces and topped with crushed nori and dried bonito flakes. It was quite a sight, but the taste and texture were even more amazing: rich, thick, custard-like, both sweet and savory, and so delicious!

Furikake is a Japanese seasoning usually made up of shredded toasted nori, toasted sesame seeds, and sea salt. You can find it (as well as okonomiyaki sauce) in the Asian aisle of well-stocked supermarkets, in most Asian markets, or online.

Combine the cabbage, carrot, and green onions in a large bowl and toss to mix well.

In a second smaller bowl, whisk together the flour, eggs, dashi, salt, and pepper. Stir in the shrimp. Pour the egg mixture over the cabbage and toss to coat the vegetables evenly.

Heat the oil in an 8-inch skillet over medium heat. When the oil is hot, pour the entire vegetable mixture, including all of the liquid, into the skillet and cook for 7 to 8 minutes, until the pancake is mostly set. Using a wide spatula, carefully flip the pancake and cook for 4 to 6 minutes longer, until golden brown and fully set.

Transfer the pancake to a large plate and let cool for 5 minutes. Decorate the pancake with squiggles of okonomiyaki sauce and mayonnaise, a sprinkling of furikake, and finally bonito flakes. Cut into 8 wedges and serve immediately.

POACHED YOLK-STUFFED RAVIOLI

8 ounces Basic Egg Pasta Dough (page 19)

Fresh flat-leaf parsley leaves, for pasta

Semolina flour, for dusting

½ cup whole milk ricotta cheese

¼ cup mascarpone cheese, at room temperature

1 medium egg yolk, lightly beaten

3 tablespoons grated Parmesan cheese

1 tablespoon minced fresh thyme

2 teaspoons thinly sliced fresh chives

1 clove garlic, minced

Salt and freshly ground black pepper

1 (750 ml) bottle Pinot Grigio wine

4 thyme sprigs

2 cups heavy cream

1 cup cold unsalted butter, cut into cubes

Grated zest and juice of 1 orange

Grated zest and juice of 1 lemon

Salt and freshly ground black pepper

20 quail egg yolks

1 chicken egg, whisked with 2 tablespoons water

Grated Parmesan cheese

Grated lemon and orange zest

Fresh thyme leaves

I had this amazing pasta dish at L'Atelier de Joël Robuchon in London: just four ravioli. As I cut one open, I was delighted to see a yolk run out. It was instantly memorable, and the yolk gave a creamy texture to the pasta. We've added herbs to the pasta dough in our version, an easy way to transform it from plain to stunning. - Teri

On a lightly floured work surface, roll out the pasta dough into a paper-thin sheet about 12 inches long and 24 inches wide. Cut the sheet lengthwise into strips 6 inches wide. You should have 4 strips. Top one-third of the strips with 2 rows of parsley leaves. Top each parsley-topped strip with a plain pasta strip. Roll out the stacked strips until they are paper-thin and the parsley leaves are encased in the dough. Gently toss the pasta with semolina and cover with plastic wrap until ready to use.

To make the filling, combine the ricotta, mascarpone, egg yolk, Parmesan, thyme, chives, and garlic in a bowl and mix well. Season with salt and pepper and set aside.

To make the beurre blanc, combine the wine and thyme in a saucepan and bring to a simmer over medium heat. Simmer for 12 to 15 minutes until reduced to ⅔ cup. Stir in the cream and continue to simmer until reduced to 1 cup. Whisk in the butter, a few cubes at a time, until all of it has been incorporated. The sauce should thicken enough to coat the back of a wooden spoon. Add the orange and the lemon zest and juice, mixing well, and season with salt and pepper. Set aside and keep warm in a water bath until ready to use.

To fill the ravioli, lay the pasta strips flat on a work surface and brush away any excess semolina. Place tablespoon-sized dollops of filling every 2 inches along the length of two of the strips, making 12 mounds in all. Using the back of a teaspoon, create a hollow in each mound of filling and carefully place a quail yolk in each hollow. Brush the egg and water mixture on the dough surrounding each mound. Carefully lay a second pasta strip over the top and gently press around each mound to release any air bubbles and seal the ravioli. Center a 2-inch round cutter around each mound to cut out the ravioli. You should have 20.

Fill a large stockpot three-quarters full of salted water and bring to a boil over high heat. Gently slide the ravioli into the boiling water and cook at a gentle boil for 3 minutes, just enough to cook them through; the pasta will become opaque. Using a slotted spoon, retrieve the ravioli and divide them evenly among 4 plates.

Divide the warm sauce evenly among the ravioli, spooning it over the top. Garnish each serving with the Parmesan, lemon and orange zest, and thyme leaves and serve immediately.

ROASTED BONE MARROW

8 (3- to 4-inch-long) marrowbones, preferably center cut

Salt and freshly ground black pepper

8 quail eggs

4 radishes, trimmed and thinly sliced

¼ cup loosely packed microgreens

Sourdough toast points, for serving

It wasn't until I was in culinary school that I began a serious flirtation with bone marrow. Sure, I had found it in my braised shanks. But in school, we used it in a variety of applications. We created sauces from the roasted marrow as well as added it to our vegetable purees for a touch of sticky richness. Today my favorite way to enjoy bone marrow is roasted with salt and pepper and smeared onto toast points. Here, we've amplified our marrow with fried quail eggs for an extra-decadent, special treat. - Jenny

Place marrow bones in a large bowl of salted, cold water for 2 hours to draw out any blood and impurities that may remain. Remove the bones from the water, gently rinse and pat dry.

Preheat the oven to 450°F. Place the marrowbones, cut side up, on a baking sheet. Season with salt and pepper. Roast for 15 to 20 minutes, until the marrow softens but has not melted.

Fry the quail eggs in butter (as directed on page 12) for about 2 minutes or until the white turns opaque and the edges begin to crisp and turn golden brown.

Arrange the roasted marrowbones on a platter and top with the fried eggs, then top the bones with the radishes and microgreens. Arrange the toast points on the platter and serve immediately.

SPAETZLE WITH SWEDISH MEATBALLS

MEATBALLS

2 slices country
white bread

⅓ cup whole milk

2 tablespoons extra-
virgin olive oil

¼ yellow onion,
finely diced

1 clove garlic, minced

1 teaspoon smoked
paprika

¼ teaspoon
ground cumin

¼ teaspoon freshly
grated nutmeg

8 ounces ground beef

8 ounces ground turkey

1 egg, lightly beaten

1 teaspoon salt

½ teaspoon freshly
ground black pepper

2½ tablespoons
unsalted butter

SAUCE

2 tablespoons all-
purpose flour

1 cup beef stock

⅓ to ½ cup heavy cream

1 tablespoon minced
fresh oregano

Salt and freshly ground
black pepper

The handmade German pasta called spaetzle is easy to make. You can use a specially designed spaetzle maker, which forces the dough through holes into boiling water, or you can press the dough through a colander with a rubber spatula. It's hard to beat spaetzle on its own, buttery and crisp around the edges and seasoned with salt and pepper. Here, we've paired it with Swedish meatballs for a hearty meal.

To make the meatballs, put the bread in a bowl, pour in the milk, and set aside to soak.

Heat the oil in a skillet over medium-high heat. Add the onion and sauté for 2 to 3 minutes, until translucent. Add the garlic, paprika, cumin, and nutmeg and sauté for 1 minute longer. Remove the skillet from the heat and stir in the soaked bread with any milk remaining in the bowl. Stir in the beef, turkey, egg, salt, and pepper, mixing gently to combine the ingredients thoroughly without overworking them. Cover the bowl and refrigerate the meatball mixture for at least 30 minutes or for up to 24 hours.

Form the chilled meat into about 24 balls, using 2 tablespoons for each ball. To cook the meatballs, melt the butter in a large skillet over medium-high heat. Add all of the meatballs in a single layer and cook, turning the balls as needed, for 2 to 3 minutes, until browned on all sides. Lower the heat to medium and cook for 4 to 5 minutes, until the meatballs are cooked though (cut into a meatball to check). Transfer the meatballs to a bowl and season them lightly with salt and pepper.

To make the sauce, return the skillet to medium-high heat, stir the flour into any fat and browned bits remaining in the skillet, and cook, stirring, for 2 to 3 minutes to cook off the raw-flour taste. While whisking constantly, pour in the stock in a steady stream and then simmer, stirring constantly, for 2 to 3 minutes, until the sauce thickens. Stir in the cream and then the oregano. Season with salt and pepper.

Return the meatballs to the skillet with the sauce and hold over the lowest heat while you prepare the spaetzle.

To make the spaetzle, whisk together the flour and salt in a bowl. In a second smaller bowl, whisk together the eggs, milk, and 1 tablespoon of melted butter. Pour the egg mixture into the flour mixture and whisk until smooth.

(ingridients and method continue on the next page)

SPAETZLE WITH SWEDISH MEATBALLS (continued)

SPAETZLE

2¼ cups all-purpose flour

½ teaspoon salt

3 eggs

1 cup whole milk

1 tablespoon unsalted butter, melted and cooled, plus 3 tablespoons

Salt and freshly ground black pepper

Fill a large pot three-fourths full with salted water and bring to a boil over high heat. Using a spaetzle maker or a colander and a firm rubber spatula, push the batter through the holes into the water and boil for 3 to 4 minutes, just until the spaetzle float. Using a slotted spoon, lift the spaetzle from the water, draining well, and transfer to a bowl.

Melt the remaining 3 tablespoons of butter in a large skillet over medium-high heat. Add the spaetzle and cook, stirring gently, for 4 to 5 minutes, until lightly browned and slightly crisp. Season lightly with salt and pepper.

To serve, divide the spaetzle evenly among 4 broad, shallow bowls. Top with the meatballs and sauce and serve immediately.

SAVORY STRATA

2 tablespoons unsalted butter, at room temperature

3½ tablespoons canola oil

1½ cups diced smoked ham

1 small yellow onion, diced

2 cloves garlic, minced

12 shiitake mushrooms, stems discarded and caps thinly sliced

Salt and freshly ground black pepper

1 cup chopped broccolini

2 green onions, white and green parts, thinly sliced

1 tablespoon minced fresh thyme

6 eggs

1 cup whole milk

1 cup shredded white Cheddar cheese

¼ cup grated Parmesan cheese

2 tablespoons whole-grain mustard

2 teaspoons hot sauce

1½ teaspoons salt

½ teaspoon freshly ground black pepper

10 slices Hawaiian sweet bread, each about 3 by 5 inches

2 ripe tomatoes, thinly sliced

This hearty dish, made by layering bread with eggs, cheese, vegetables, and other ingredients, makes a great cozy-night-at-home dinner. We call for slices of Hawaiian sweet bread, but you can instead cube or slice our Hawaiian Sweet Rolls (page 27). The leftovers from this dish are wonderful to have on hand, because they are the kind you can grab straight out of the fridge and eat.

Preheat the oven to 375°F. Use the butter to generously grease a 9-inch round baking dish that is about 2½ inches deep.

Heat 1 tablespoon of the oil in a large skillet over medium-high heat. Add the ham and sauté for 3 to 4 minutes, until lightly seared. Transfer to a bowl and set aside.

With the skillet still over medium-high heat, add 1½ tablespoons of the oil and then add the onion and garlic and sauté for 4 to 5 minutes, until translucent and fragrant. Add the mushrooms and continue to sauté for 4 to 5 minutes, until mushrooms are seared on each side. Season with salt and pepper and transfer the vegetables to the bowl with the ham.

Add the remaining 1 tablespoon of oil to the skillet over medium-high heat and then add the broccolini and sauté for 4 to 5 minutes, until softened. Stir in the green onions and thyme and then transfer to the bowl with the ham and vegetables. Stir the ham and the vegetables together, distributing all of the ingredients evenly.

In a second bowl, whisk together the eggs, milk, Cheddar, Parmesan, mustard, hot sauce, salt, and pepper.

Sprinkle two-thirds of the ham and vegetable mixture evenly over the bottom of the prepared baking dish. Dip the bread slices into the egg mixture and arrange them in a spiral pattern on top of the ham and vegetable mixture. Top the bread with the tomato slices and then distribute the remaining ham and vegetable mixture evenly over the tomatoes. Finally, pour any remaining egg mixture evenly over the top.

Cover the dish with aluminum foil and bake for 25 minutes. Uncover and continue to bake for 25 to 30 minutes, until the strata is cooked through (a paring knife inserted into the center should come out clean) and golden brown on top. Let cool for 5 to 10 minutes before cutting and serving.

PASTA CARBONARA

2½ teaspoons salt

1 pound dried cavatelli pasta (or pasta of your choice)

1 egg

3 egg yolks

¾ cup grated Parmesan cheese, plus more for garnish

½ teaspoon salt

½ teaspoon freshly ground black pepper

4 ounces pancetta, diced

We make this simple pasta for lunch in the studio when we're craving something rich and creamy, but it's equally welcome at home on the dinner table. We generally have all of the ingredients on hand, which makes it easy to whip it up. We crank up the heat at the end to ever so slightly scramble the eggs in the sauce, but that's just us! Try it our way if you wish, or keep the heat low to blanket the pasta with the creamiest sauce.

Fill a large pot three-fourths full with water, add 2 teaspoons salt and bring to a boil over high heat. Stir in the pasta and boil for 6 to 8 minutes, until al dente. Drain, reserving ½ cup of the pasta water.

While the pasta is cooking, whisk together the egg, egg yolks, Parmesan, remaining ½ teaspoon salt, and pepper in a bowl.

Place a large skillet over medium heat, add the pancetta, and sauté for 5 to 6 minutes, until golden brown and crisp. Drain off all but 2 tablespoons of the fat from the skillet (discard or save for another use) and reserve the skillet with the pancetta in it.

Whisk the pasta water into the egg mixture. Return the skillet to medium heat and stir in the drained pasta, coating it evenly with the pancetta and fat. Turn down the heat to low, pour the egg mixture over the pasta, and stir gently to coat the pasta evenly with the egg mixture. Continue to cook, stirring, for about 3 minutes, until the sauce thickens. Season with salt and pepper.

Divide the pasta evenly among 4 warmed, shallow bowls. Top each serving with a little Parmesan, season with salt and pepper, and serve immediately.

TIP: For a thicker sauce, stir in additional grated Parmesan and cook until you achieve the desired consistency.

GREEN ONION FRIED BLACK RICE

1 cup black rice

2 cups chicken stock
or water

6 eggs

2 tablespoons
vegetable oil

1 tablespoon toasted
sesame oil

2 cloves garlic, minced

1 teaspoon peeled and
minced fresh ginger

Salt and freshly ground
black pepper

2 green onions, thinly
sliced, for garnish

1 teaspoon sesame
seeds, toasted, for
garnish

I've had black forbidden rice only a handful of times, and each time I've been blown away. The rice is fragrant and delicate and deliciously soaks up any surrounding flavors. We have deliberately prepared this dish simply in order to highlight the black rice—and then we topped it with a fried egg, of course. - Jenny

Rinse the rice in three or four changes of water and then let it drain thoroughly in a fine-mesh sieve. Transfer the rice to a saucepan, add the stock, and bring to a boil over high heat. Cover, lower the heat to a brisk simmer, and cook for about 20 minutes, until the rice is tender and no liquid remains in the pan. Remove from the heat, uncover, and fluff the rice with a fork. Set aside.

Whisk 2 of the eggs in a small bowl. Heat the vegetable oil and sesame oil in a wok or large skillet over high heat. Add the beaten eggs and cook through, until they just set, gently breaking them up into large pieces as they cook. Add the garlic, ginger, and cooked rice, season with salt and pepper, and continue to stir and toss for 3 to 4 minutes, until some of the rice becomes crispy. Remove the rice from the heat and divide evenly among 4 bowls. Keep warm.

Fry the remaining 4 eggs as directed on page 12 (using oil instead of butter).

Place an egg on top of each bowl of rice. Season the eggs lightly with salt and pepper, garnish with the green onions and sesame seeds, and serve immediately.

TIP: When shopping for black rice for this recipe, be sure to buy regular rice rather than glutinous or sticky rice, such as black rice from the Manipur region of India. Glutinous rice will clump too much when it is fried. Forbidden Rice from Lotus Foods, available in well-stocked supermarkets and specialty food stores, is a good choice. You can also find black rice at most Asian markets or online.

SWEETS

CREAMY LEMON CURD TART

CRUST

32 to 36 shortbread cookies, crushed into fine crumbs

6 tablespoons unsalted butter, melted

LEMON CURD

1 egg, at room temperature

3 egg yolks, at room temperature

1 cup superfine sugar

Grated zest of 2 lemons

⅔ cup freshly squeezed lemon juice

½ teaspoon pure vanilla extract

6 tablespoons unsalted butter, cut into small cubes

1 cup heavy cream

MERINGUE TOPPING

3 egg whites, at room temperature

½ teaspoon cream of tartar

½ teaspoon pure vanilla extract

1 cup superfine sugar

Thin lemon slices, for garnish

Fresh mint leaves, for garnish

We like this tart year-round, whether to cool down a hot summer evening or to take advantage of abundant winter citrus. You can leave the soft meringue topping as is or torch it lightly for a more rustic finish.

Preheat the oven to 375°F.

To make the crust, stir together the cookie crumbs and melted butter in a bowl, moistening the crumbs evenly. Transfer the mixture to a 10-inch fluted tart pan with a removable bottom and press evenly onto the bottom and sides.

Bake for 25 to 30 minutes, until toasted and fragrant. Let cool completely on a wire rack.

To make the lemon curd, whisk together the egg, egg yolks, sugar, lemon zest and juice, and vanilla in a bowl. Transfer the mixture to a saucepan, place over medium-low heat, and bring to a simmer, whisking constantly for 5 to 7 minutes, until the mixture thickens enough to coat the back of a wooden spoon and holds a trail drawn by a fingertip. Remove from the heat and strain through a fine-mesh sieve into a bowl. Stir in the butter, a cube or two at a time, until fully incorporated.

Prepare an ice-water bath and then nest the bowl of curd in the bath. Let the curd cool completely, stirring it occasionally and taking care not to slosh any ice water into it.

Pour the cream into a bowl and beat with a stand mixer or handheld mixer on medium-high speed, or by hand with a whisk, until firm peaks form. Using a rubber spatula, fold the whipped cream into the cooled curd until fully incorporated and no white streaks are visible.

Scrape the curd into the cooled crust and smooth the top. Refrigerate the tart for at least 1 hour, until the curd is fully set.

To make the topping, use a stand or handheld mixer to beat the egg whites in a clean bowl with a clean whip attachment at medium speed until light and frothy. Add the cream of tartar and vanilla and continue beating until soft peaks form. With the mixer running, add the sugar, a few tablespoons at a time, until all of the sugar is incorporated and the whites are thick, glossy, and hold medium-firm peaks.

Let the tart ring drop away from the pan base, remove the pan base from the tart by running an offset spatula between the bottom of the tart and top of the pan base, then transfer the tart to a serving plate. Using a large spatula, top the tart with a couple mounds of prepared meringue. Then gently spread the whites decoratively over the filling, being careful not to deflate the whites. Decorate with lemon slices and mint leaves.

SPICY CHOCOLATE MOUSSE

4 ounces Mexican chocolate, chopped

6 ounces bittersweet chocolate (60 percent cacao), chopped

¾ cup unsalted butter

⅓ cup strong brewed coffee

3 duck eggs, separated, or 5 chicken eggs, separated

¾ cup plus 2 tablespoons superfine sugar

½ teaspoon ground cinnamon

¼ teaspoon chile powder

2½ tablespoons coffee liqueur

1 teaspoon pure vanilla extract

½ teaspoon salt

Whipped cream, for garnish

Shaved bittersweet chocolate, for garnish

Chocolate mousse tastes best when it is light and airy. We've dressed up our version with a good-quality cinnamon and chile-laced Mexican chocolate (Ibarra is a popular brand sold in the states) and then added strong brewed coffee for a deeper flavor and a little chile powder for some spicy heat. The whipped cream and shaved chocolate are the grand finale to this rich and creamy dessert.

Combine the Mexican and bittersweet chocolates, the butter, and the coffee in the top pan of a double boiler. Place it over (not touching) gently simmering water in the lower pan (or rest a heatproof bowl in the rim of a saucepan of simmering water). Heat, stirring occasionally, until the chocolate and butter melt and the mixture is smooth. Remove from the heat.

In a second double boiler, whisk together the egg yolks, sugar, cinnamon, chile powder, liqueur, vanilla, and salt in the top pan. Place over (not touching) gently simmering water in the lower pan and whisk until the yolks are pale yellow and fluffy. Gently fold the chocolate mixture into the yolk mixture, then set aside, off the heat.

Put the egg whites in a bowl and beat with a stand mixer or handheld mixer on medium-high speed, or by hand with a whisk, until firm peaks form. Using a rubber spatula, gently fold the whites into the chocolate-yolk mixture just until evenly incorporated and no white streaks are visible.

Spoon the mixture into a piping bag fitted with a large plain tip (about 1 inch), or into a gallon-sized resealable plastic bag with a corner snipped off to create a 1-inch opening. Pipe the mousse into four (8-ounce) dessert glasses, dividing it evenly and filling each glass half to three-fourths full. Refrigerate for at least 4 hours, until the mousse sets and is well chilled, or for up to 36 hours.

To serve, garnish each mousse with a dollop of whipped cream and a sprinkling of shaved chocolate.

BRICK TOAST

½ cup unsalted butter, at room temperature

2 tablespoons superfine sugar

1 duck egg yolk, or 2 medium chicken egg yolks

½ cup plus 2 tablespoons sweetened condensed milk

½ teaspoon pure vanilla extract

¼ teaspoon salt

4 slices Pullman bread, each 2 inches thick

Everyone should experience this simple, delicious dessert at least once. Brick toast is a thick slice from a Pullman loaf (a big, square loaf) that is first marked with cross-hatching and then smothered with a sweet custard and baked until toasted and caramelized. I love nibbling on sugary pieces of this sweet, crisp toasted bread on its own or dipping it in coffee. My guy prefers to eat his like a funnel cake: topped with ice cream, whipped cream, chocolate or caramel sauce, sliced strawberries, and crowned with a maraschino cherry. I'm thinking brick toast ice cream sandwiches might be something that needs to happen. It sounds almost too good to be true . . . almost. - Jenny

Preheat the oven to 350°F. Line a baking sheet with a parchment paper.

Cream together the butter and sugar in a bowl with a wooden spoon. Add the egg yolk and stir until well mixed. Stir in the milk, vanilla, and salt until fully incorporated.

Place the bread slices on a work surface, and score each slice in a 1-inch cross-hatch pattern, cutting deeply but not completely through the bread. Spread the bread slices generously with the butter mixture, allowing it to seep into the scoring. (You will not need all of the butter mixture. Store the remainder in an airtight container in the refrigerator for up to 2 weeks.)

Arrange the slices, buttered side up, on the prepared baking sheet and bake for 14 to 16 minutes, until golden brown. Let cool for 5 minutes before serving.

VANILLA BEAN SEMIFREDDO BARS

3 cups heavy cream

1¼ cups superfine sugar

1 vanilla bean,
halved lengthwise,
seeds scraped out
and pod discarded

6 egg yolks

1 pound bittersweet
chocolate (60 percent
cacao), chopped

1½ cups crushed toasted
hazelnuts

Semifreddo is like easy ice cream: all the flavor and texture with half the fuss. We use our semifreddo to make my favorite frozen treat: hand-dipped ice cream bars. You will need 8 Popsicle sticks. - Jenny

Whisk together the cream, ¾ cup of the sugar, and vanilla seeds in a bowl. Whip the cream mixture with a stand mixer on medium-high speed, or with a whisk by hand, until firm peaks form. Cover and refrigerate while you prepare the yolks.

Rinse the mixer beater or hand whisk. Combine the egg yolks and the remaining sugar in a bowl and beat with the stand mixer on medium-high speed, or with the whisk by hand, for 4 to 6 minutes, until fluffy and pale yellow. Fold the whipped cream into the yolk mixture until fully incorporated.

Line a 9-by 13-inch baking pan with plastic wrap, allowing it to overhang the sides by a few inches. Spread the mixture evenly in the pan. Cover with the overhanging plastic wrap and freeze for 9 to 10 hours, until completely frozen.

Put the chocolate in the top pan of a double boiler and place over gently simmering water in the lower pan (or rest a heatproof bowl in the rim of a saucepan). Heat, stirring occasionally, until the chocolate melts completely. Remove from the heat, let cool slightly, then pour into a tall, narrow heatproof jar or glass. The chocolate should still be melted, but barely warm to the touch when you begin to dip the bars. Place melted chocolate into a warm water bath to keep it from solidifying.

Use the plastic wrap to lift the semifreddo from the baking pan to a work surface. Using a large, sharp knife, cut the semifreddo lengthwise into 3 equal strips and then crosswise into 4 equal strips, to make 12 bars total.

Line a baking sheet with parchment paper or a silicone baking mat. Have 8 Popsicle sticks ready. Dip one-third of a Popsicle stick into the melted chocolate, insert the chocolate-coated portion into one end of a semifreddo bar, and place on the prepared baking sheet. Repeat with the remaining sticks and semifreddo bars. Return the bars to the freezer for at least 30 minutes, until completely firm.

Place hazelnuts in a large, shallow dish. Retrieve a bar from the freezer and dip it into the melted chocolate to cover it completely, or brush the melted chocolate over the surface of the bar. Working quickly before the chocolate sets, dredge the bar in the crushed hazelnuts, then return the bar to the baking sheet in the freezer. Repeat to coat the remaining bars.

Freeze the bars for at least 30 minutes, then wrap them individually in plastic wrap and return to the freezer. They will keep for up to 2 weeks.

PAVLOVA WITH CRÈME ANGLAISE AND BERRIES

MERINGUE SHELL

4 egg whites

1 teaspoon pure
vanilla extract

1¼ cups superfine sugar

1 tablespoon cornstarch

TOPPING

3 cups mixed
fresh berries (such
as raspberries,
blueberries, and
blackberries)

¼ cup superfine sugar

2 tablespoons freshly
squeezed lemon juice

½ cup heavy cream,
whipped to stiff peaks

⅔ cup Crème Anglaise
(page 17)

Pavlova is a wonderful showcase for complementary and contrasting textures. The best part is cracking through the crispy meringue shell with your spoon to find its airy pudding-like center and then scooping up a billowy cloud of whipped cream along with sweet-tart berries and rich crème anglaise. We especially like to serve this Pavlova at picnics and other warm-weather get-togethers when fresh berries are in season.

To make the shell, preheat the oven to 325°F. Line a baking sheet with parchment paper.

Using a stand mixer or a handheld mixer, beat the egg whites in a clean bowl with a clean whip attachment at medium speed until light and frothy. Add the vanilla and mix briefly. With the mixer running, add the sugar, a few tablespoons at a time, until the whites are thick and glossy and hold medium-firm peaks. Using a rubber spatula, fold in the cornstarch just until incorporated.

Scoop out the meringue onto the center of the prepared baking sheet and form a 6- to 7-inch round with a bowl-shaped hollow about 4 inches wide in the center.

Put the baking sheet into the oven and immediately lower the temperature to 300°F. Bake for 1 hour and then turn off the oven; leave the shell in the oven for 1 to 2 hours, until completely cool.

To make the filling, toss the berries with the sugar and lemon juice in a bowl, gently mashing the berries just a bit. Let stand for at least 1 hour or for up to 2 hours.

To serve, transfer the meringue shell to a serving plate. Fill the center with whipped cream and drizzle the crème anglaise over the cream. Scoop the berries over the cream and serve immediately.

QUINDIM

2 tablespoons unsalted butter, melted and cooled, plus 2 tablespoons for the pan

2 cups superfine sugar, plus 4 tablespoons for the pan

1 cup unsweetened dried coconut

¼ teaspoon salt

2 cups superfine sugar

12 egg yolks

1 cup full-fat canned coconut milk

When I was in Brazil, I saw these bright yellow custards everywhere. Although I don't have the biggest sweet tooth, I also knew I couldn't leave the country without indulging in what seemed to be a seriously popular dessert. One happy sugar coma later, I had gobbled down a single large quindim by myself. This simple baked custard packs loads of flavor with the taste of a sweet coconut crème brûlée and the texture of thick a lemon curd. Pair it with a strong cup of freshly brewed coffee. - Jenny

Preheat the oven to 350°F. Brush 12 wells of a standard muffin pan with butter, and then coat with superfine sugar and tap out the excess.

Toss together the coconut and salt in a bowl. In the bowl of a stand mixer fitted with the paddle attachment or in a large bowl with a handheld mixer, combine the melted butter, egg yolks, and sugar and beat on medium speed for about 4 minutes, until pale yellow and fluffy. Add the coconut milk and mix until combined. Finally, add the sugar-coconut mixture and mix on medium speed until fully combined.

Ladle the custard into the prepared muffin wells, filling them to the rim. Carefully transfer the muffin pan to a large baking pan the same depth as the muffin pan. Pull out the center oven rack, put the baking pan on the rack, and then carefully pour hot water into the baking pan to reach halfway up the sides of the muffin pan.

Bake for 20 to 25 minutes, until the custards are mostly set but still a bit wobbly in the center.

Carefully remove the baking pan from the oven, and then carefully pull the muffin pan from the water bath. Run a small, thin-bladed knife or small offset spatula around the edge of each custard to release it from the pan sides. Let cool for 10 minutes and then invert the pan onto a clean cutting board, lined with plastic wrap, to unmold the custards and carefully lift off the pan. Let cool completely before transferring into individual liners and serving.

Quindim will keep in an airtight container in the refrigerator for up to 3 days.

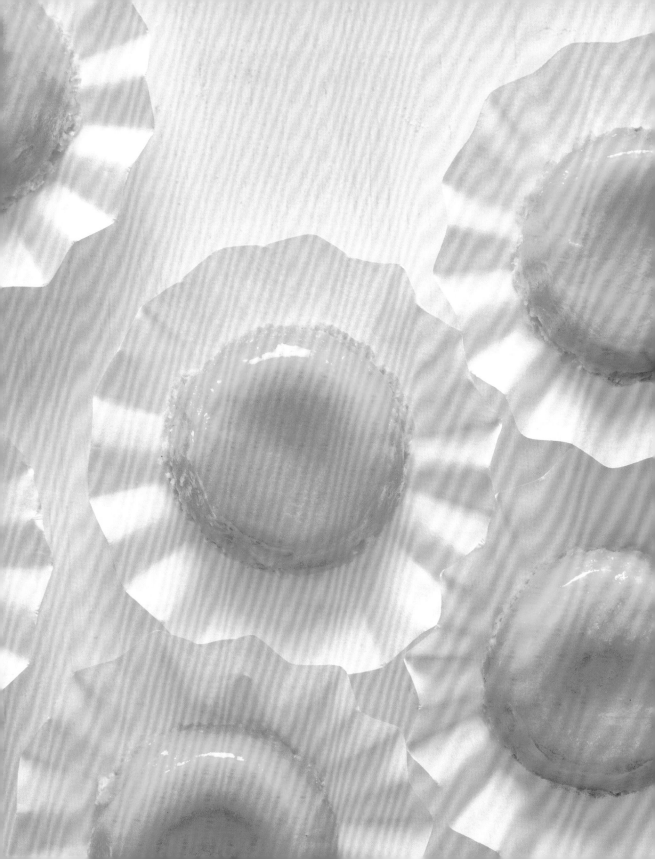

CRÈME BRÛLÉE

3 cups heavy cream

1 cup superfine sugar

1 vanilla bean, halved lengthwise

5 egg yolks

¼ cup turbinado sugar

The charm of eating crème brûlée lies in cracking through the thin, brittle caramelized sugar surface to reach the cool, creamy custard below. I crack through that topping mindfully, attempting to shatter it into as many small shards as possible. This allows me to enjoy the contrast of crunchy sugar and creamy custard in every bite. Although the dessert seems complicated and sophisticated, the recipe is astonishingly easy. If you don't have a kitchen torch, you will need to spring for one to caramelize the sugar properly, but the irresistible hard caramel topping is worth the expense. - Teri

Preheat the oven to 325°F. Position an oven rack in the lower third of the oven.

Stir together the cream and ½ cup of the superfine sugar in a saucepan. Using the tip of a knife, scrape the vanilla seeds from inside the pod halves and add them to the pan along with the pod halves. Place over medium-low heat and bring to a simmer, whisking constantly. Retrieve and discard the vanilla pod halves or rinse thoroughly and save for another use. Remove from the heat.

Whisk together the egg yolks with the remaining ½ cup of superfine sugar in a heatproof bowl until light and pale yellow. Pour about one-third of the hot cream mixture (about 1 cup) into the yolks in a slow, steady stream while whisking constantly. Return the yolk-cream mixture to the saucepan, return the pan to medium-low heat, and cook, whisking constantly, for 3 to 4 minutes, until the mixture thickens slightly.

Remove from the heat and strain the custard through a fine-mesh sieve into a heatproof bowl. Ladle the custard into four 8-ounce ramekins, dividing it evenly. Carefully transfer the ramekins to a baking pan. Pull out the oven rack, put the baking pan on the rack, and then carefully pour hot water into the pan to reach two-thirds of the way up the sides of the ramekins.

Bake for 40 to 50 minutes, until the custards are mostly set but still a bit wobbly in the center.

Carefully remove the baking pan from the oven, and then carefully remove the custards from the water bath. Let the custards cool for about 1 hour, then cover and refrigerate for about 1 hour, until cold, or for up to 3 days.

To serve, sprinkle 1 tablespoon of the turbinado sugar evenly over the top of each custard. Slowly wave a kitchen torch back and forth over the sugar on each custard until it melts and changes color. Let the custards sit just until the sugar hardens, then serve immediately.

CHOCOLATE-DIPPED COCONUT-PECAN MACAROON BARS

½ cup oat flour

3¼ cups (about 14-ounces) unsweetened, shredded dried coconut

1 cup chopped pecans

¾ teaspoon sea salt

1 (14-ounce) can sweetened condensed milk

1½ teaspoons pure vanilla extract

2 egg whites, at room temperature, beaten until frothy

12 ounces bittersweet chocolate (60 percent cacao), chopped

French-style filled *macarons* have become trendy, but I usually prefer a good old coconut macaroon. I find the crispy exterior yielding to a soft, chewy interior addictive. We've transformed that classic into a snackable bar, dipped in chocolate and finished with a sprinkle of sea salt. The bars are not only great for dessert but also with your morning coffee or milk. Yes, it is sometimes nice to start off the day with something extra sweet! - Jenny

Preheat the oven to 350°F. Line a 9-by 13-inch pan with parchment paper.

Toss together in a bowl the oat flour, coconut, ⅔ cup of the pecans, and ¼ teaspoon of the salt. Add the milk, vanilla, and egg whites and stir until evenly mixed.

Transfer the coconut mixture to the prepared pan and press in an even layer onto the bottom. Sprinkle the remaining ⅓ cup pecans evenly over the top. Using a sharp knife, score the surface lengthwise down the center to make 2 equal strips. Then score crosswise in 12 equal strips, to make 24 bars total. Do not cut through to the pan.

Bake for 25 to 30 minutes, until golden brown. Remove the pan from the oven and, using the score marks as a guide, cut into 24 bars. Let cool completely in the pan on a wire rack, about 1½ hours.

Put the chocolate in the top pan of a double boiler and place over (not touching) gently simmering water in the lower pan (or rest a heatproof bowl in the rim of a saucepan of gently simmering water). Heat, stirring occasionally, until the chocolate melts and is smooth. Remove from the heat, let cool slightly, and then transfer to a long and narrow heatproof container. The chocolate should be only slightly warm to the touch when dipping the bars.

Line a baking sheet with parchment paper. Carefully remove the bars from the baking pan. Dip a bar into the melted and cooled chocolate, covering about half of the bar and shaking off the excess chocolate back into the bowl. Then place on the prepared baking sheet. Sprinkle the bar lightly with salt before the chocolate dries. Dip and salt the remaining bars the same way, using the remaining ½ teaspoon of salt for all of the bars.

Let the chocolate dry completely, about 2 hours, before serving. To store, layer the bars in an airtight container, separating the layers with parchment paper or waxed paper, and keep in a cool, dry place for up to 5 days.

PEACHES 'N' CREAM CAKE

PEACHES

1 cup superfine sugar

1 cup water

½ cup honey

Juice of ½ lemon

1 cinnamon stick

1 star anise pod

4 firm, ripe yellow peaches, halved, pitted, and each cut into 8 wedges

CAKE

2½ cups cake flour

1¾ cups superfine sugar

2½ teaspoons baking powder

½ teaspoon salt

½ cup unsalted butter, at room temperature

1 egg, lightly beaten

3 egg whites, lightly beaten

¾ cup sour cream

¾ cup whole milk

1 teaspoon pure vanilla extract

1 teaspoon almond extract

Grated zest of 1 lemon

WHIPPED CREAM

2 cups heavy cream

⅔ cup superfine sugar

1 vanilla bean, split lengthwise

Fresh sage leaves, for garnish (optional)

With four egg whites and just one yolk, this cake has a delicate, airy texture that pairs nicely with rich whipped cream and fresh peaches simmered in honey syrup. We like it best with a big scoop of vanilla ice cream alongside.

To make the peaches, combine the sugar, water, honey, lemon, cinnamon, and star anise in a saucepan over medium-low heat. Heat, stirring occasionally, until the sugar dissolves. Stir in the peaches and simmer, stirring occasionally, for about 5 minutes, until softened and glazed, but not falling apart. Remove from the heat and set aside.

To make the cake, preheat the oven to 350°F. Line the bottoms of 2 (9-inch) round cake pans with parchment paper, then lightly butter the parchment and the sides of the pans.

Whisk together the flour, sugar, baking powder, and salt in a bowl. Add the butter and mix with a wooden spoon until the mixture is evenly crumbly. Add the egg and egg whites and mix until fully incorporated. Stir in the sour cream, milk, vanilla and almond extracts, and lemon zest until well mixed, thick, and smooth.

Divide the batter evenly between the prepared pans. Bake for 20 to 22 minutes, until the cakes just begin to brown and a toothpick inserted into the center comes out clean. Let the cakes cool completely in their pans on wire racks, at least 1 hour.

To make the whipped cream, whisk together the cream and sugar in a bowl. Using the tip of a knife, scrape the vanilla seeds from inside each pod half and add them to the bowl. Whip the cream mixture with a stand mixer or handheld mixer on medium-high speed, or with a whisk by hand, until firm peaks form.

To finish the cake, run a thin-bladed knife around the inside edge of a cake pan to loosen the cake, then invert the cake onto the wire rack, lift off the pan, and peel off the parchment. Repeat with the second pan. Using a long, serrated knife, cut each cake layer in half horizontally to make 4 layers total. Place 1 layer on a serving platter and spread one-fourth of the cream evenly over the layer. Repeat with the remaining 3 layers and the remaining cream. Spoon the peaches over the cream on the top layer. Garnish with the sage leaves and serve.

FOI THONG

3 duck egg yolks

2 chicken egg yolks

2 cups water

3 cups superfine sugar

½ cup honey

1 teaspoon jasmine extract (optional)

2 tablespoons black sesame seeds, for garnish (optional)

In this Thai dessert, strands of golden egg yolk are poached in a sweet sugar-honey syrup and then gathered up into a nest of sugared threads. These nests are often used to top cakes or are served alongside fruit in syrup.

Whisk together the duck and chicken egg yolks in a bowl. Press through a fine-mesh sieve into a resealable plastic bag.

Set a wire rack over a baking sheet. Combine the water, sugar, honey, and jasmine extract in a wide saucepan and bring to a boil over medium-high heat, stirring until the sugar dissolves. Snip one corner off the plastic bag to make a ⅛-inch opening. While moving the bag in a circular motion over the boiling sugar-water mixture, press out one-fourth of the yolks in a thin, steady stream. Set the bag aside.

Using 2 forks, gently gather together the sugared yolk threads to create a small bundle, then transfer the bundle to the wire rack. Top with 1½ teaspoons of the sesame seeds. Repeat three more times with the remaining yolk mixture and sesame seeds to form 4 bundles total.

Let the bundles dry and cool completely, about 1 hour, before serving.

GRAPEFRUIT-POPPY SEED POUND CAKE

2 cups all-purpose flour

1 teaspoon
baking powder

½ teaspoon salt

¼ teaspoon
ground cinnamon

1 cup unsalted butter, at
room temperature

1½ cups superfine sugar

2 eggs, lightly beaten

2 egg yolks,
lightly beaten

1 cup plain whole-fat
Greek yogurt

Grated zest and juice
of 1 grapefruit
(about ½ cup juice)

½ teaspoon pure
vanilla extract

1 tablespoon
poppy seeds

Sweets were not regularly kept on hand in my childhood home, and cake or pie was rarely, if ever, served. Instead, our family meals ended with big plates of cut fruit. But we did always have one sweet in the house: pound cake. I'm not sure why it was the one exception, but there always seemed to be a loaf in the kitchen. It was not regarded as dessert, however, but rather as something to snack on during the day, evidenced by how it would steadily shrink from morning to night. Lemon–poppy seed pound cake was my favorite for its tartness and the crunch of the seeds. Here we use grapefruit in place of the lemon for a sweet and subtly fragrant flavor. It's what I think of as my childhood dessert, even if that is not the way we ate it. - Jenny

Preheat the oven to 350°F. Line a 9 by 5-inch loaf pan with parchment paper.

Whisk together the flour, baking powder, salt, and cinnamon in a bowl. In a second bowl, cream together the butter and sugar with a wooden spoon until pale yellow and fluffy. Add the eggs and egg yolks, stirring well. Stir in the yogurt until fully incorporated and then fold in the flour mixture until incorporated. Stir in the grapefruit zest and juice, vanilla, and poppy seeds just until combined.

Spread the batter evenly in the prepared pan. Bake for 1½ to 1¾ hours, until a toothpick inserted into the center comes out clean. Let cool completely in the pan on a wire rack, about 1 hour, before unmolding, slicing, and serving.

CHOCOLATE-ORANGE SOUFFLÉ

2 tablespoons unsalted
butter, at room
temperature

¼ cup plus 3 tablespoons
superfine sugar

¾ cup whole milk

2 egg yolks,
at room temperature

1½ tablespoons
almond meal

Grated zest and juice
of 1 orange (about
⅔ cup juice)

5 ounces bittersweet
chocolate, melted
and cooled

4 egg whites,
at room temperature

Confectioners' sugar,
for garnish

Grated orange zest,
for garnish

Soufflés can be intimidating—even terrifying—to make. The place most people tend to go wrong is with the egg whites. But if you follow the instructions here for whipping the whites and folding them gently into the batter—and don't overthink what you are doing—your soufflés are guaranteed to please the fussiest French chef.

Preheat the oven to 350°F. Generously coat four 6-ounce ramekins with the butter, then coat them with 2 tablespoons of the sugar, tapping out the excess.

Combine the milk and 1 tablespoon of the sugar in a small saucepan and bring to a simmer over medium-low heat. Set aside, off the heat.

Whisk together the egg yolks, almond meal, and remaining ¼ cup of sugar for about 3 minutes, until pale yellow and fluffy. Whisk in the orange zest and juice until fully incorporated. Slowly add 3 to 4 tablespoons of the hot milk mixture into the yolk mixture in a slow, steady stream while whisking constantly. Return the yolk-milk mixture to the saucepan, return the pan to low heat, and cook, whisking constantly, for 3 to 4 minutes, until the mixture thickens enough to coat the back of a wooden spoon. Remove from the heat and stir in the melted chocolate. Let the mixture cool completely.

Put the egg whites in a bowl and beat with a stand mixer or handheld mixer on medium-high speed, or by hand with a whisk, until firm peaks form. Using a rubber spatula, gently fold the whites into the chocolate-yolk mixture just until evenly incorporated and no white streaks are visible.

Divide the mixture evenly among the prepared ramekins, filling them almost to the rim. Place the ramekins in a baking pan. Pull out the center oven rack, put the baking pan on the rack, and then carefully pour hot water into the baking pan to reach halfway up the sides of the ramekins.

Bake for 15 to 20 minutes, until the soufflés have risen significantly. Remove from the oven and top each soufflé with a light dusting of confectioners' sugar and a light grating of orange zest. Serve immediately.

CRANBERRY CORNMEAL COOKIES

¾ cup bread flour

½ cup plus
2½ tablespoons
stone-ground yellow
cornmeal

½ teaspoon
baking powder

¼ teaspoon baking soda

¼ teaspoon salt

½ cup unsalted butter,
at room temperature

½ cup superfine sugar

½ cup honey

1 duck egg, lightly
beaten, or 2 medium
chicken eggs, lightly
beaten

1 teaspoon pure vanilla
extract

¾ cup dried cranberries

When it comes to corn bread, I prefer a savory one. It's not that I don't like sweet corn bread—I do—but let's call a cake a cake: you need to frost it and then, if it is a special day, stick a candle in it. What I really love is the taste of honey-laced cornmeal in this chewy cookie, dotted with sweet-tart cranberries and crisp cornmeal bits. The bread flour ensures a chewy cookie, but if you don't have any on hand, all-purpose flour will work fine. - Jenny

Whisk together the flour, cornmeal, baking powder, baking soda, and salt in a bowl.

In a second bowl, combine the butter, sugar, and honey, and cream them together with a wooden spoon until lighter in color and fluffy. Scrape down the sides of the bowl with a spatula and mix in the egg and vanilla until smooth. Then add the flour mixture and stir until evenly combined. Fold in the cranberries. Cover and refrigerate for 30 minutes to 1 hour.

Preheat the oven to 350°F. Line a baking sheet with parchment paper.

For each cookie, scoop up about 2 tablespoons of the dough and place on the prepared baking sheet, spacing the cookies about 1½ inches apart.

Bake for 12 to 14 minutes, until the cookies just start to brown around the edges. Transfer them to a wire rack and let cool for at least 15 minutes before serving.

To store the cookies, let cool completely, then layer them in an airtight container, separating the layers with parchment paper or waxed paper, and keep at room temperature for up to 5 days.

BEIGNETS

⅔ cup lukewarm water (110°F)

3 tablespoons superfine sugar

2½ teaspoons active dry yeast

1 duck egg, lightly beaten, or 2 medium chicken eggs, lightly beaten

½ cup evaporated milk (not sweetened)

4 tablespoons unsalted butter, at room temperature

½ teaspoon ground cinnamon

½ teaspoon salt

3½ cups bread flour

Peanut oil, for deep-frying

½ cup confectioners' sugar, for dusting

Whether plain or stuffed with a compote, beignets are a delicious treat. That said, it's hard to go wrong with sweetened deep-fried dough. A friend who shares my admiration for fried dough once suggested that peanut oil produces the lightest, nuttiest beignets. After trying it, I agree, and it's now the only oil I use for frying any sweet dough. - Jenny

Stir together the water and superfine sugar in a large bowl. Sprinkle the yeast evenly over the top and let stand for about 5 minutes, until foamy.

Stir the egg, milk, butter, cinnamon, and salt into the yeast mixture, mixing well. Add the flour, ½ cup at a time, mixing well after each addition until fully incorporated. With the final addition, mix until a soft, and slightly sticky dough forms.

Lightly flour a work surface. Turn the dough out onto the floured surface and knead for 4 to 6 minutes, until smooth and soft. Lightly oil a large bowl, transfer the dough to it, and turn the ball to coat the surface with oil. Cover the bowl with a damp kitchen towel and let the dough rise at warm room temperature for about 1 hour, until doubled in size.

Lightly flour a work surface and then punch down the dough and turn it out onto the floured surface. Cut the dough in half and form each half into a ball. Keep 1 ball covered with a damp towel or loosely covered with plastic wrap while you work with the other ball on the floured surface. Roll out the dough into a rectangle 12 by 18 inches and about ⅛ inch thick. Cut the dough in a crosshatch pattern to make 13 to 14 diamonds, each about 1½ inchs lengthwise and 1 inch crosswise. Repeat with the second ball of dough.

To fry the beignets, pour the oil into a deep pot to a depth of 3 inches and heat to 350°F. Line a plate with paper towels and place near the stove.

Gently lower 5 to 6 pieces of dough into the hot oil and fry, turning them once, for 3 to 4 minutes, until golden all over. Using a slotted spoon, transfer to the paper-lined plate to drain. Repeat with the remaining dough.

Sift the confectioners' sugar generously over the beignets and serve immediately.

DOBOS TORTE

SPONGE CAKE

⅔ cup unsalted butter, at room temperature

½ cup granulated sugar

6 eggs, separated

½ cup all-purpose flour, sifted

⅔ cup confectioners' sugar, sifted

1½ teaspoons pure vanilla extract

COFFEE BUTTERCREAM

1 cup granulated sugar

3 tablespoons water

2 tablespoons light corn syrup

6 egg yolks

1 pound cold unsalted butter, cut into 2-tablespoon pieces

1½ tablespoons coffee extract

1 cup strong brewed coffee

⅔ cup superfine sugar, for topping

Dobos torte is traditionally made up of thin layers of sponge cake spread with chocolate buttercream and then finished with caramel on top. My favorite thing about our version of the decadent torte is a toss-up between all the thin layers of cake and the delicious coffee buttercream. It takes a few steps and quite a bit of time to assemble this rich, showy dessert, but all of your hard work will be rewarded when you serve it. - Jenny

Preheat the oven to 325°F. Line 2 large baking sheets (13 x 18 inch half sheet pans) with parchment paper and lightly butter the parchment.

To make the cake, combine the butter and granulated sugar in a bowl and cream together with a wooden spoon or with a handheld mixer or stand mixer, fitted with a paddle attachment, until pale yellow and fluffy. Add the egg yolks, one at a time, mixing well and scraping down the sides of the bowl after each addition. Carefully stir the flour into the egg yolk mixture, mixing just until combined. Set aside.

Place the egg whites in a clean bowl and beat with a whisk. Once the egg whites are frothy, add the confectioners' sugar, a little at a time, while whisking constantly. When all of the sugar has been incorporated, add the vanilla and continue to whisk until stiff peaks form.

Stir 1 cup of the egg whites into the yolk mixture until well mixed. Fold in the remaining egg whites just until combined and no white streaks are visible.

Divide the egg mixture evenly between the prepared baking sheets and, using an offset spatula, spread in a thin layer. Bake for 30 to 35 minutes, until golden brown. Let cool completely on the pans on wire racks.

To make the buttercream, combine the granulated sugar, water, and corn syrup in a small saucepan over medium heat. Heat, stirring occasionally with a wooden spoon, until the sugar dissolves. Raise the heat to high and cook at a vigorous boil, without stirring, until thick and smooth and a candy thermo-meter reads 240°F.

Meanwhile, place the egg yolks in a bowl and whisk together for about 4 minutes or use a handheld mixer or stand mixer with a paddle attachment, until pale yellow and fluffy. When the sugar syrup is ready, remove from the heat. While whisking vigorously (so the yolks don't scramble), pour the sugar mixture into the whipped yolks in a slow, steady stream.

(continues on the next page)

As soon as all of the sugar syrup has been incorporated, begin adding the butter, one piece at a time, beating until each piece is incorporated before adding the next one. Continue whipping until all of the butter has been added and the mixture is light, fluffy, and smooth. Fold in the coffee extract just until combined. Set aside until ready to use.

Use a sharp knife, cut the cooled cake on each pan into 4 equal rectangles, each 4 by 9 inches, saving the scraps. Gently peel the cakes from the parchment. Place a small dot of buttercream onto the center of a cake stand or other serving plate and center a cake rectangle on the dot. Set aside about ⅔ of the buttercream to use for frosting the cake. Using a pastry brush, dab the surface of the rectangle with a small amount of the brewed coffee to moisten and flavor the cake. Using a small offset spatula, spread a thin, even layer of the buttercream over the cake and then top with another cake rectangle. Repeat with the remaining cake rectangles, coffee, and buttercream until you have an 8-layer cake. Place small strips of parchment under about 1 inch of the cake and onto the surface of the plate or cake stand until it is completely covered with parchment Using some of the reserved buttercream, spread a thin crumb coat of buttercream on the sides and top of the cake.

Place the cake in the refrigerator to chill for about 2 hours. Remove from the refrigerator, frost the sides, and top with the remaining buttercream.

To make the caramel topping, cut the reserved cake scraps into different-size circles, ranging from 1½ inches to ½ inch in diameter. Arrange the circles on a baking sheet lined with parchment and set aside. Melt the superfine sugar in a small, heavy saucepan over medium heat until it is evenly melted and turns a caramel color (about 340 to 350°F). Remove from the heat and quickly but carefully spoon the caramel over the cake disks, coating them thinly and evenly.

When the caramel hardens, arrange the disks atop the cake, pressing them gently into the buttercream to secure, and then serve.

FROZEN CUSTARD

2 cups cold heavy cream

1 cup cold half-and-half or whole milk

1 cup superfine sugar

1 vanilla bean, halved lengthwise

12 egg yolks

½ teaspoon salt

I grew up in the Midwest, so frozen custard was my ice cream. What's the difference between the two? Frozen custard is extra rich and creamy because it uses a greater proportion of egg yolks and has a higher butterfat content. I made many visits to Culver's, a frozen custard and fast-food restaurant chain, during the hot, sticky summers of my adolescence. This vanilla bean–flavored recipe—and our variations (page 163)—are just enough to satisfy my cravings until my next trip to the Midwest. - Jenny

Stir together the cream, half-and-half, and ½ cup of the sugar in a saucepan. Using the tip of a knife, scrape the vanilla seeds from inside 1 pod half and add them and the pod half to the pan. Place over medium-low heat and cook, stirring constantly, until the sugar dissolves and small bubbles form around the sides of the pan. Remove from the heat.

Whisk together the egg yolks, the remaining ½ cup of sugar, and the salt in a heatproof bowl for 3 to 5 minutes, until pale yellow and fluffy. Pour one-third of the hot cream mixture (about 1 cup) into the yolk mixture in a slow, steady stream while whisking constantly. Return the yolk-cream mixture to the saucepan, return the pan to medium-low heat, and cook, whisking constantly, for 3 to 4 minutes, until the mixture thickens enough to coat the back of a wooden spoon.

Prepare an ice-water bath. Line a sieve with cheesecloth and strain the custard through the sieve into a clean bowl. Nest the bowl in the ice-water bath, then scrape the vanilla seeds from inside the remaining pod half, stir them into the custard, and then add the pod half. Let the custard cool completely, stirring it occasionally and taking care not to slosh any ice water into it.

Tightly cover the custard with plastic wrap and refrigerate until very cold, at least 8 hours or up to overnight.

Remove the vanilla bean pod half from the custard, then transfer the custard to an ice cream maker and freeze according to the manufacturer's instructions. Scoop the custard into small glass jars (so that when the custard is frozen, you have ready-to-go individual servings; you can also transfer the frozen custard into a large airtight, freezer-proof container) and place in the freezer for 3 to 5 hours, until firm, before serving.

(continues on the next page)

MATCHA & BLACK SESAME

CAKE BUTTER

CHOCOLATE

VANILLA BEAN

SALTED CARAMEL

RASPBERRY & COCONUT

STRACCIATELLA

BLACKBERRY & MERLOT

COFFEE

VARIATIONS:

MATCHA & BLACK SESAME: Stir 2½ teaspoons matcha (green tea powder) into the cream and half-and-half mixture before heating on the stove top. Stir 3 tablespoons crushed black sesame seeds into the frozen custard mixture halfway through the churning process in the ice cream maker.

CAKE BATTER: Replace the vanilla bean with 1 tablespoon of pure vanilla extract, adding it to the custard base right before pouring the mixture into the ice cream maker. Stir 1 cup yellow cake mix into the custard base before chilling and then churning in the ice cream maker.

CHOCOLATE: Stir ⅔ cup natural unsweetened cocoa powder into the cream and half-and-half mixture before heating on the stove top.

SALTED CARAMEL: Put 1 cup sugar, 1 tablespoon water, and 1 tablespoon light corn syrup in a saucepan and place over medium-high heat. Do not stir. When the sugar melts and turns amber, after 10 to 15 minutes, remove the pan from the heat and stir in ⅔ cup heavy cream (be careful, the mixture will bubble up). Then add 1½ tablespoons sea salt and 2 teaspoons pure vanilla extract and stir until smooth. Allow caramel to cool completely. Stir the caramel into the custard base before chilling.

RASPBERRY & COCONUT: Replace the 1 cup half-and-half and 1 cup of the heavy cream with 2 cups full-fat canned coconut milk. Stir 1½ cups lightly crushed fresh raspberries into the frozen custard mixture halfway through the churning process in the ice cream maker.

STRACCIATELLA: Drizzle ⅔ cup melted bittersweet chocolate into the frozen custard mixture halfway through the churning process in the ice cream maker.

BLACKBERRY & MERLOT: Puree 1½ cups fresh blackberries and strain through a fine-mesh sieve. Stir together the berry puree, 1 tablespoon confectioners' sugar, and ½ cup Merlot. Stir the blackberry mixture into the chilled custard base just before churning in the ice cream maker.

COFFEE: Stir 1¼ cups strong brewed coffee, chilled, into the chilled custard base before churning in the ice cream maker.

ACKNOWLEDGMENTS

We would like to start by giving a huge bear hug to our agent, Carole Bidnick, without whom this book would never have been made. Thank you for always being so positive and for understanding us. No words can describe how much we appreciate you! Thank you to Anne Park, for taking the time out of your schedule to lend us your beautiful hands. You have helped to make our book come to life, and we are deeply grateful. We also want to send a giant thank you to Kaitlin Ketchum, our editor, and Tatiana Pavlova, our designer. You both made this process so easy for us, even when we were at our most difficult. You guys are the best. To Serena Sigona and Erin Welke, the two people who helped make this book beautiful and put it into the hands of the right people: A great team came together to make this book. We are so dang lucky!

FROM TERI

Thank you to Don, who has long been a guiding force and has always given me the best advice anyone could hope for in life. Thank you to my mom, for always being supportive, and to my dad, Lori, and my strange and unusual sisters, for making our recipes and sending me pictures—love you guys! To Grandpa and Granna, I love you both more than words can say. Your support and knowledge have helped me be a better person. To Nika and Karin, love you both like family, always.

FROM JENNY

Thank you to my family, for their love and encouragement as I continue on my weird journey through the food world. I love you for being my rock since day one, and I feel incredibly lucky to have you all in my life. Thank you to my main man, Jordan, for putting up with things, like too many nights of me cooking bacon at 2:00 a.m. when I am prepping for a shoot, and for always trying to put a smile on my face—you big ole ham! I love you. Thank you to Dexter, the little guy that pulls on my heartstrings every day, for all of the cuddles and sweet memories these past few years. You really do make my world a better place! Thank you to my beautiful and supportive friends, for being some of the most honest and willing taste-testing participants and for always calling me your "most successful friend." You ladies really know how to take the humble right outta me (wink)! Finally, thank you to Denise and Cindie, the two women who introduced me to this crazy world of food styling and recipe development. I will be forever grateful that you took me, a totally naïve to food-styling girl from the Midwest, under your wings and taught me the ins and outs of the business.

INDEX

FROM TERI

To Jim Fisher, who will never get to see this book, but who
I know would be proud of me.

FROM JENNY

To Mom, Dad, Jordan, and Anne who kept me going
throughout this journey with their endless positivity and love.

All rights reserved.
Published in the United States by Ten Speed Press, an imprint of the Crown Publishing Group,
a division of Random House LLC, a Penguin Random House Company, New York.
www.crownpublishing.com
www.tenspeed.com

Ten Speed Press and the Ten Speed Press colophon are registered trademarks of Random House LLC.

Library of Congress Cataloging-in-Publication Data
Fisher, Teri Lyn.
The perfect egg : a fresh take on recipes for morning, noon, and night / Teri Lyn Fisher, Jenny Park.
     pages cm
  1. Cooking (Eggs) I. Park, Jenny (Jenny S.) II. Title.
  TX745.F57 2015
  641.6'75--dc23
                    2014030803

Hardcover ISBN: 978-1-60774-625-6
eBook ISBN: 978-1-60774-626-3

Printed in China

Design by Tracy White Taylor and Tatiana Pavlova

10 9 8 7 6 5 4 3 2 1

First Edition

MEASUREMENT CONVERSION CHARTS

VOLUME

U.S.	IMPERIAL	METRIC
1 tablespoon	½ fl oz	15 ml
2 tablespoons	1 fl oz	30 ml
¼ cup	2 fl oz	60 ml
⅓ cup	3 fl oz	90 ml
½ cup	4 fl oz	120 ml
⅔ cup	5 fl oz (¼ pint)	150 ml
¾ cup	6 fl oz	180 ml
1 cup	8 fl oz (⅓ pint)	240 ml
1¼ cups	10 fl oz (½ pint)	300 ml
2 cups (1 pint)	16 fl oz (⅔ pint)	480 ml
2½ cups	20 fl oz (1 pint)	600 ml
1 quart	32 fl oz (1⅔ pints)	1 l

TEMPERATURE

FAHRENHEIT	CELSIUS/GAS MARK
250°F	120°C/gas mark ½
275°F	135°C/gas mark 1
300°F	150°C/gas mark 2
325°F	160°C/gas mark 3
350°F	175 or 180°C/gas mark 4
375°F	190°C/gas mark 5
400°F	200°C/gas mark 6
425°F	220°C/gas mark 7
450°F	230°C/gas mark 8
475°F	245°C/gas mark 9
500°F	260°C

LENGTH

INCH	METRIC
¼ inch	6 mm
½ inch	1.25 cm
¾ inch	2 cm
1 inch	2.5 cm
6 inches (½ foot)	15 cm
12 inches (1 foot)	30 cm

WEIGHT

U.S./IMPERIAL	METRIC
½ oz	15 g
1 oz	30 g
2 oz	60 g
¼ lb	115 g
⅓ lb	150 g
½ lb	225 g
¾ lb	350 g
1 lb	450 g